CARMODY & BLIGHT:
The Dialogues

New and Selected

CARMODY: *There was just something magnificent about glorifying the leader.*

BLIGHT: *He's the guy standing on the rock?*

CHARLES D. TARLTON

Carmody & Blight: The Dialogues
New and Selected Poetry and Prose
By Charles D. Tarlton

ISBN: 978-0-9980375-7-8

Library of Congress Control Number: 2019914085

Publication Date: October 2019

Published by KYSO Flash Press: http://www.kysoflash.com
Bellingham, Washington, USA. Printed in the USA

Prosimetra (tanka prose), poems, and stories published in this collection are copyrighted by Charles D. Tarlton. All rights reserved.

This book was designed, edited, and produced by Clare MacQueen. The KYSO Flash logo is copyrighted © 2015 by Clare MacQueen and was designed in collaboration with James Fancher. All rights reserved.

The background image on the covers, *Wisps Surrounding the Horsehead Nebula*, is copyrighted © 2012 by Star Shadows Remote Observatory (SSRO). All rights reserved. Image is reproduced here with kind permission from Rick Gilbert, SSRO co-founder and webmaster. For more information, see page 183 herein (End Notes: Credits: Visual Images).

The title-page image, *Hail Caesar* (photographer unknown), depicts five "Romans" in 1957, college students who were cheerleaders at the University of California, Riverside (UCR). At far right stands Charles D. Tarlton (known in those days as Chuck Tarlton). Photograph is reproduced herein with his permission from page 31 of UCR's 1957 yearbook, *The Tartan*.

Except for short quotations within critical articles or reviews, no portion of this book, including its covers, may be used, reproduced, or transmitted in any form or by any means, electronic or mechanical, including photocopying and recording, or by any information storage or retrieval system, without permission in writing from the copyright holders.

Please send any questions and comments to the Publisher:

KYSOWebmaster@gmail.com

To James W. Percey, Jr.,
my lifelong best friend. I miss him.

CARMODY: *When one of us is gone, what do you think the other will do?*

BLIGHT: *Well, for one thing, try not to think about it.*

Also by Charles D. Tarlton

Get Up and Dance
Dance Poems
With cover art by Ann Knickerbocker
KYSO Flash Press (2019)

Touching Fire:
New and Selected Ekphrastic Prosimetra
With art by Ann Knickerbocker and 25 others
KYSO Flash Press (2018)

Una Vida de Piedra y de Palabra
Number 23 in the 2River Chapbook Series
http://www.2river.org/chapbooks/tarlton/default.html
(May 2010)

Fortune's circle: A Biographical
Interpretation of Niccolo Machiavelli
Quadrangle Books (1970)

Table of Contents

11	**Part I**
13	By the Light of the Moon
14	#1: *"We need a map..."*
15	#2: *"I think the world must be coming to an end..."*
16	#3: *"Wasn't it true, Plato asked..."*
17	#4: *"You say, we've got nothing to say..."*
18	#5: *"These voices you're talking about..."*
19	#6: *"I was waiting, you know..."*
20	#7: *"Did you hear the veil is lifting..."*
21	#8: *"How long has that birdfeeder been empty..."*
22	Allusory
25	#9: *"Think of something..."*
26	#10: *"When you look at a painting..."*
27	#11: *"What did you say..."*
28	#12: Sympathy
30	#13: *"I am looking inside for inspiration..."*
31	#14: *"What did you learn today?"*
32	#15: *"Hypothetically speaking..."*
33	#16: *"It's exhilarating!"*
34	You Have to Get Loose
35	#17: *"I am an old man to be fooling around..."*
36	#18: *"I had another friend once..."*
37	#19: *"Your endless arguments..."*
38	#20: *"These identical redwoods side by side..."*
39	Ways of Transfiguration
42	#21: *"It's a thick line between art and life..."*
44	#22: *"Please, don't just make up stuff..."*
45	#23: *"They say you can't write poetry..."*
46	#24: *"Ah, the light at the end of the tunnel..."*
47	#25: *"I think this is about as far as we dare..."*
48	#26: *"We may have left them alone..."*
49	#27: *"There are no strangers on this street..."*
50	Crépescule
52	#28: *"My management principles do not include..."*

53	#29: "I'm never anywhere I want to be…"
54	#30: "I am exactly like a helium balloon…"
55	#31: "Perhaps only the ancient thinkers…"
56	#32: "We were laughing loudly all the way…"
57	**Part II**
59	In the Groove
60	#33: "Into the alabasters/ And night blues…"
62	#34: "Why are you standing there?"
63	#35: "Just the littlest bit…"
64	#36: "I just love the look…"
65	#37: "Men were there, bearded and dirty…"
66	#38: "When you have counted out the syllables…"
67	Conundrum
68	#40: "One thing I've learned…"
69	#41: "The big picture, you know…"
70	#42: "What does it matter?"
71	#43: "Never joke about money…"
72	#44: "Do you think you could stand…"
74	#45: "Someone I used to know…"
75	#46: "Tell me, how well did you know…"
76	#47: "You know, I don't feel a day older…"
77	Masters of Illusion
78	#48: "Oh, Vanity!"
79	#49: "And then, bango!…"
80	#50: "Are you feeling any wiser now…"
81	#51: "There is a moment when…"
82	#52: "Here's the situation…"
83	#53: "This is what we might call the scene…"
84	A Question of Murder
86	#54: "Get inside the conventions…"
87	#55: "I know! I know how to do it!…"
88	#56: "Imagine dinner for three…"
89	#57: "A rich man strolls by…"
90	#58: "Locale is everything…"
91	#59: "I'm right on the verge…"

92	Substitute
93	#60: "*Swift the river, swiftly towards…*"
94	#61: "*No more!…*"
95	#62: "*I dreamed about playing…*"
96	#63: "*Abracadabra!…*"
97	Psychotherapeutics

99	**Part III**
101	*L'Art de la guerre*
102	Stereotypicals
103	#64: "*What do they get out of just mixing…*"
104	#65: "*Listen! Listen! After each roar…*"
106	#66: "*I want to talk about each…*"
107	Talking to Myself
108	#67: "*The rhetorical fervor rises…*"
109	#68: "*The trouble with making plans…*"
110	Richard Diebenkorn: Three Ekphrastic Moments: Preface
	Ocean Park #116 (1979)
	Ocean Park #118 (1980)
115	#69: "*None of my questions have answers…*"
117	#70: "*It presses on a nerve whenever…*"
118	#71: "*Sometimes I feel so…*"
119	*Le verbe être*
120	#72: "*Give your life a name then…*"
121	#73: "*At the end of the whole thing…*"
122	#74: "*Something so beautiful it was frightening?*"
124	#75: "*All the words connected loosely…*"
125	By Their Fruits
127	From the Doctor's Rough Drafts
128	In the Garden of Delights
130	#76: "*Sit down with the animals…*"
131	Trained Seals
133	#79: "*What I do not want are any courageous…*"
134	#80: "*I started out thinking I'd give them…*"

135	At Carmody's Bar Waiting for Ezra Pound: A Theatrical:
	(3) Up Close and Personal
	(4) Time, Gentlemen, Time
	(7) On the Scent
	(8) Out of the Fog
	(10) Have We Learned Anything?
147	End of the Line
148	#81: Pushing the Paint Around
150	Along the Gallery Wall: A Review
152	#82: "*If you want to know, I'm simply bored...*"
153	#83: "*I'm so sick of people talking...*"
154	Eight Episodes in the Saga of Carmody & Blight
158	Crossroads
161	**Part IV: A Dozen Dialogues on Dying**
163	#84: "*It's taken such a long time to grow this old...*"
164	#85: "*I'm afraid of blood...*"
165	#86: "*Life and death, immortality and hereafter...*"
166	#87: "*Do you know the worst thing?*"
167	#88: "*What must seem enormous...*"
168	#89: "*In a moment bright as a bubble...*"
169	#90: "*Death and his desperate little partners...*"
170	#91: "*If I were dying, I wouldn't want to know...*"
171	#92: "*What interests me is the way...*"
172	#93: "*Did you ever think...*"
173	#94: "*Death is so final it erases all the worry...*"
174	Quietus
175	**End Notes**
177	About the Author
179	Credits

✧

Part I

in the kitchen
heated transformations
rising biscuits
the crisped skin of roast chicken
cold butter on the tongue

[…]

CARMODY: *You know, sometimes my moods just rise and fall like the flags up there on the two hotels; a little wind and my flags are up!*

BLIGHT: *We'll be sailing in and out of the doldrums together.*

By the Light of the Moon

CARMODY: *What direction is the moon?*

BLIGHT: *North by up?*

There were no streetlights on the highway for about two miles across the sandy river-wash, so he sped up and was going sixty-five when he passed the California Highway Patrol cruiser parked off the road in the dark.

He saw the police headlights come on just after he went by, but instead of slowing down he kept going, where the road curved off to the left. Still no lights in his rear-view mirror, so he took a sharp right turn into a little road and switched off his headlights.

He watched the cop go by in the mirror and, then, just as he turned his headlights back on, he saw the cul-de-sac come to an end. The upcoming curbs looked several feet tall and he slammed on the brakes. The tires shrieked, the car swerved, and then went into a full brodie skid, ending up facing backwards in the middle of the road.

The lights in several houses switched on, then porch lights, and, finally, several people came out to see what had happened.

"You all right?" a man in pajamas hollered over to him.

He had crossed his arms on the steering wheel and leaned his head on his arms. His heart was pounding.

"Want us to call the police?" a nice woman called out to him. "They could be here in a minute."

✧

#1

CARMODY: *We need a map, that's all I'm saying. We go this way and we go that, but we never get anywhere.*

BLIGHT: *Why aren't we making a map?*

I was searching for a metaphor to capture the idea that the same human traits that draw us together in love, in clubs, in society itself could also drive us apart. I pushed the button, there was an audible click, and on the screen over my head there suddenly appeared a close-up slide of an aboriginal cedar-bark basket. "*E pluribus unum*," I declared.

they named him Zeus
this boy born in Fresno
his father worked
in the cotton fields, pruned grapes
had higher expectations

what time is it
on the antique Bulova
both hands at two
where the universe rubs
against itself at the edge

my life's story
undergoes retelling
with each failure
switches tracks each derailing
eyes on the horizon

✧

#2

CARMODY: *I think the world must be coming to an end. Look at it!*

BLIGHT: *I can't bear to look at it.*

If you walk down to the edge of the sea in winter, down to where the cold waves finally stop and turn around, hissing in the sand—the indifference will get into you. The waves lift up, they come to the edge of the sand, they flatten, and they slide back down. The sea swallows them, only to send new swollen undulations onto the sand, over and over. The sea and the waves have seen everything.

logical flaws
reproducing mutations
scratched matrices
mistakes made manifest
in later generations

dialectics
turn questions and answers
into progress
a soft hand in a hard place
moves us to the next level

after today
what happens cannot be
known. The future
is always empty, just
out in front a little way

#3

CARMODY: [Reading.] *Wasn't it true, Plato asked, that the body has less of truth and essence than the soul?*

BLIGHT: [Aside.] *He's going somewhere with this. It doesn't just stop here.*

"My soul, my soul!" As if there was a difference between me, and my soul. To commemorate the soiling of their souls, the girls in my Catholic school would tie little paper ribbons in their hair, one for each venial sin. In the end, it actually became a kind of competition among them—who would have the most ribbons.

sails in the wind
swell and blow in the idea
of push and shove
the shapes the canvas takes
surfaces, lines, and the air

the absolute
encompasses everything
all the details
cancel out, the common good
where your best interest lies

kids on the street
some Arab, some Mexican
fumble English
vowels, miss their *esses*
as they try to fit in

✧

#4

CARMODY: *You say, we've got nothing to say. You say, it's all been said; there's no saying anything new.*

BLIGHT: *What I'm saying is that even if we found something new, what would it matter? We have nothing decisive to say, that's what I mean.*

At every art show this year, it was the same thing. There are apparently only two kinds of painters who get to exhibit—those who have torn off their own skin in the effort to find something "different" (literally, one painter had first laid on layers of glued paper and paint and then sanded off random portions of it) and those who first draw conventional forms (a nude, a barn, a seascape) and then make it orange where it ought to be green, blue where it ought to be red, and so on. At the end of modern Art's bloodline, there's only hemorrhaging.

I heard that voice
agonizing in the night
down in the street
someone hurls a bottle
makes a brutal music

it was her back
arched, the breasts lifting up
you can't fool me
no matter how abstractly
painted, those are her thighs

many futures
are conceived, die stillborn
scattered around
we kick through them like dead leaves
on our way to sponsored forms

✧

#5

CARMODY: *These voices you're talking about... maybe you want to hear them as if they came from outside... just maybe, you understand... because otherwise, it would be you thinking those thoughts.*

BLIGHT: *You just listen to them!* [Pause, then in a slightly changed voice.] *"So, you think we're saying too much? Well, don't blame us."* [In a second, entirely different voice.] *"Yeah, don't try to blame us!"*

Those things in my field of vision that look like X-rayed hairs or maybe translucent paramecia under the microscope are called "floaters." They are, in reality, signs of physical degeneration in the vitreous humour, but they are experienced as objects suspended in liquid or in the air. Try as we might, we cannot look directly at them; they are in the eye itself. The instrument we're looking at is the object we're looking *with*.

thoughts in the air
where everyone's insisting
truth escapes us—
so, we turn a blind eye
dodging culpability

the hand is quick-
er than the wasted glance
blinking, blinking
under hot lamps, halogen-quartz
she smiles for her swan song

philosophy
shows us the only way out
where we're drowning
these elaborate puzzles
mean nothing once they're solved

✧

#6

CARMODY: *I was waiting, you know, but everything else kept moving; the clock was the first thing I noticed, then the little wind in the pollarded limbs. I could feel the world around me pushing along, going on ahead.*

BLIGHT: *Did you say anything?* [Pause. Impatiently.] *What did you say?*

Early on a rainy summer morning, a man in a yellow slicker parked his bicycle on the 11th Street freeway overpass. He looked down into the oncoming traffic heading to New York or the shore, scrutinizing the faces of as many of the drivers passing under him as he could. His eyes went back and forth trying to make contact.

doctors elude
death routinely, in a day
oncology
in one hospital wing
pediatrics opposite

the principle
of loss is factored into
calculations
of the intensity
of even happiness

I never dream
about my dead father
I'm more likely
to go to sea when I sleep
worry about missing clothes

✧

#7

CARMODY: *Did you hear the veil is lifting? Apotheosis! It will be the end of everything.*

BLIGHT: *I think you mean Apocalypse, but hey, nothing lasts forever.*

We cowered in bed the whole night the *tempête* raged outside. The sound of the wind was deafening, like a jet engine parked outside, and the house rumbled and shook. In the morning, all five roads out of the village were blocked by fallen trees and the roof had been blown off the ancient bread oven on the square. It's only a cliché, I know, but right then you couldn't hear a sound.

sans-abrisme
cold alone no fixed abode
ancien flâneur
trying to imagine
staying in the moment

sayings about
the glass half empty or full
the sands of Time
now I can see death ahead
it won't be much longer now

little babies
in grocery carts or strollers
I stop and talk
miracles at the outset
I have so much to tell them

✧

#8

CARMODY: *How long has that birdfeeder been empty? Small wonder we don't hear goldfinches singing anymore.*

BLIGHT: *We could catch one and keep it in a cage.*

Here, this is exactly what I mean! This patient is obviously rigid and tense. See his lips pressing together to make a thin, hard line, and look how his shoulders are pulled up and in, you know, a barely discernible shrug. The other one is very different looking at first; he seems to be all smiles and casual gesture. But, his eyes—look at his eyes!

life in tide pools
sea anemones, mussels, and
starfish. Urchins
bathe in the slow currents, keep
their faces out of the sun

on *Queribus*
the wind blew us to our knees
outside the gate
to the inner fortress
mostly a pile of stones

he used to say
turning to my mother
as she would pay—
"I am just a kept man"
but she decided nothing

✧

Allusory

CARMODY: *You have your one good idea, for example, to make a short movie about an old French woman looking out her door. Do you just stop there? Why not another one where a man looks out, or one where a woman sticks her head in?*

BLIGHT: *Well, yes, and so on.*

If you knew the routes and schedules well enough, you could buy an Oyster pass and see every street, row, arch, arcade, square, crescent, court, mews, and woods of London. Ride each bus to the end of the line and back, switch over, grab a 17 or a 91 and climb to the upper seats. Cross the Thames, thread the narrow byways of Soho, or shade your eyes against the glitter of a Regent or Bond Street.

his proclivities
were fatherly, loved discipline
but lost his temper
punishing, turning switches
on bare legs, coat hangers

between empty tracks
that reached on parallels
to infinity
I heard his mother calling
and calling and yet calling

I lived in a town
where the days were dry and hot
in a time before
air conditioning came along
and we sweated ourselves to sleep

We were about to catch the Eurostar for Paris. I had second thoughts about traveling at 186 miles per hour and crossing under the English Channel through a tunnel, but the tickets were bought and the reservations made and maybe there would be a restaurant car or maybe I could pretend to sleep. Anyway, I have always loved trains.

memory runs into
a stone wall of what I need
just now, so I lie
say I used to be taller
and had so many more friends

could a little boy
the one who really first
experienced church
truly have grasped it all
through such experienced eyes

such venality
reflecting priestly pique
at slow old ladies
or voracity, how he
hurried to get to breakfast

Suppose all the writers up to now had fully covered everything, said all there was to say. And, further suppose you come along, doomed to re-experience all that they had known, except for this—you had to know much of it through the lens of their writings. The question here is this: do you apply your ironies to your own experiences or to those writings?

if I stood beside
the child I was now that I
am an ancient man
would I understand garbled
snatches of baby talk

could anyone speak
as children speak, see with their eyes
feel glandless passions
and report back to the world
what the rest of us forgot

I could see then just
how it had to have been, I know
things now make that so
remember tastes I can no
longer taste, vanished lightness

#9

CARMODY: *Think of something. Say something.*

BLIGHT: [Pause.] *What if I have nothing to say?*

CARMODY: *Don't try to blame any of this on me.*

BLIGHT: *The thing is, you addressed me first.*

In the fall semester, 1963, I stood in front of 463 registered students in "Introduction to the Study of Political Parties" at Berkeley. I had cribbed my lecture from an old textbook on the subject, one that the students (even the teaching assistants) would not likely know, and as I started mechanically into the first few minutes, I froze. I did not really understand what was there in the notes. I started to stammer, and then, as if returned numbly to my bed-wetting childhood, I heard myself stuttering so badly in the end that I could not say anything. I left the podium.

"Did you say all?"
in some black dream a hawk
insensibly
dark eyes and shallow, sees
everything on the surface

new poetry
sans pedigree, unrefined
speaks to itself
the lonely search for music
in deep chasms between

at his corner
filled with gesticulating rage
he wildly questions
unseen interlocutors
threatening them with his fists

✧

#10

CARMODY: *When you look at a painting and the artist is standing right there, what can you say? You know they want you to praise whatever it is, to say how powerful it is, or wonderful. But, what if you hate it?*

BLIGHT: *A sage and judicious look, a long and silent one, and then you just nod.*

Near Bolinas, California, we stopped along a country road where a ceramicist-potter had her studio in a small barn. We went inside, said hello, and walked around looking at her very interesting work. Through a window I glimpsed a large weathered brown house across a little meadow behind the barn. "Can I walk across there and look at the house?" I asked. "Sure," she said. As I approached the house behind its weathered fence, it soon became clear that it was a perfect replica of a sixteenth-century Japanese farmhouse—something straight out of a Kurosawa *samurai* movie.

perfect pencil
lines drawn across the canvas
without ruler
show faintly through painted bands
pale pastel blue and yellow

sitting, waiting
for perfection to come
knocking. Art needs
patience when conceiving
quick sure hands to make it

standing in front
of Cy Twombly's *Sesostris*
falling into
perfect colors in his lines
deliberately wild

✧

#11

CARMODY: *What did you say?*

BLIGHT: *Nothing.*

CARMODY: *Nothing?*

BLIGHT: *That's what I said!*

The law of the excluded middle makes it logically impossible for a thing both to be and not be, to exist and not exist. You know, like you can't go outside and stay in here at the same time or, try this, everything in the world is yellow except the things that aren't.

"beauty is free"
and she drew a long line
with a crayon
dividing the world in two
side by side, yellow and red

how do you bring
what is not here, in here
to wake them up
because though you can't find it
doesn't mean it is not there

exclusively
being one or the other
they come and go
leading us up to the edge
none of them looking in

✧

#12: Sympathy

CARMODY: *I was hungry, the kind of hungry you get when you're hitchhiking all day in the desert and you've got, maybe, 83¢ in your pocket.*

BLIGHT: *You were hitchhiking across the desert?*

CARMODY: [Proudly.] *On our way to a football game in Flagstaff.*

BLIGHT: *You were in college then, right?* [Pause.] *That was not serious hungry.*

We took our children to France for the summer whenever we could save up the price of plane tickets. My son, Jim, was very troubled by the people who begged money on the streets in the small towns. I made a rule then: unless beggars had lost a limb, we would ignore them. One day, in *Nogent-le-Rotrou*, we saw a man agonizing on his knees in a deep and genuine mental depression. I handed Jim a five-euro note to give the man, and I said: "That's pretty much like having your leg cut off."

facility
ease or oversimplified
pushing margins
jockeying against me
running me off the road

unrequited
disaffections doubling
helices, curved
along our moral axis
calmly winding us down

duplicity
regards itself, the cold eye's
moral focus
makes adjustments, turns the dial
pink mists top the black mountains

#13

CARMODY: *I am looking inside for inspiration, you know, for a deeper truth.*

BLIGHT: *How will you know it, I mean, how will you know it's truly inspiration?*

CARMODY: *It will be beyond my doing it, that's how!*

"The artist stands alone in relation to the world," the speaker was saying, "there can be no give and take." Let's break this down. Does he mean that the artist need not consider the world? Is that when he's embodying his vision in some medium, or when he's trying to sell the result? I wanted to write a sonnet, but I couldn't decide which of the hundreds and hundreds of years' worth of rules applied to me. I read somewhere about a poet who writes fifteen-line, unrhymed sonnets.

it has to be
serious. Integrity
doesn't really
come up when you're, say, drawing
straws for candy favors

taking a risk
that could cost you everything
because the voice
you hear inside your head
"says" it's telling the truth

what would people
say? What could you say back?
I am searching
for my own salvation
amidst the world's rubble?

✧

#14

CARMODY: *What did you learn today?*

BLIGHT: *I learned that beauty is truth, truth beauty.*

CARMODY: *Come on, be serious.*

BLIGHT: *How about this? Today's sky at sunset is spread like a Navajo sand painting in pinks and violet and gray.*

My uncle George had just come back from fighting the war in Europe; he had been a tail gunner in a B-17 and had flown more than thirty missions over Germany. He was going to junior college in Long Beach to study Art on the G.I. Bill. He taught my brother and me how to fasten a fly onto a straight pin stuck through a piece of cork and then hand the fly a quarter-inch piece of toothpick. The fly would turn it around and around like a baton twirler.

clouds needing names
run over each other
scurry under
the invisible winds
cumulus or nimbus

on the river
lily pads float just below
the wind-wrinkled
surface where our cast lures
drop and skip in the little waves

the inward eye
more than light and shadow
infects vision
with meaning. It makes us feel
what the paint intended

✧

#15

CARMODY: *Hypothetically speaking.*

BLIGHT: *And then what?*

CARMODY: *Exactly.*

He smoked two packs of unfiltered cigarettes every day of his adult life, drank whisky in the mornings, worked around the polluting oil rigs at Signal Hill for thirty years, and was partial to bacon, butter, and sweets. He died in his nineties somewhere in the Mojave. No one had the heart to perform an autopsy.

from one brush stroke
to another, piling up
figuration
in textured reds, abrupt
yellows, a long line of blue

intimidating gestures
harness our fears—this mode
of reasoning
need and *can,* modalities
prospering under the gun

in the kitchen
heated transformations
rising biscuits
the crisped skin of roast chicken
cold butter on the tongue

✧

#16

CARMODY: *It's exhilarating!* [Stands and breathes deeply, with his full chest.]

BLIGHT: *But, not hilarious?*

His daughter writes that his condition is steadily deteriorating. He cannot eat because of the cancer, so he is losing weight. Losing weight leads to postponement of his surgery. Meanwhile, he gets weaker and weaker, and has even fallen down, more than once. At a distance of three thousand miles, I am unable to connect any of this to my best friend of fifty years. I only remember the brash young scholar from Philadelphia, deliberately unwrapping and lighting his familiar cigar, poised to crush some visiting luminary's pale arguments in seminar.

these Christmas lights
reflected in dark windows
red yellow blue
blinking stars in a mirrored
sky—one symbolic angel

endless stories
as if reading from a book
each one eager
to establish worthy
bona fides, common themes

conscience[1] means two
knowing at once the same thing
in the other's
presence only one story
passes muster as truth

---

1. Author's note: From *conscire*: be (mutually aware)

✧

You Have to Get Loose

CARMODY: *I could say, "I wanted to write a poem," but someone has already said that.*

BLIGHT: *Well, Picasso and Eliot both said that it's all right to steal.*

I won't tell you how I found this red line, what it means to me sitting alone in this room. We've all had moments when things seem to cut us off and we are alone: in the night, threatened, in pain, and having our gloomiest thoughts. I imagine red, then, red everywhere, red—trees. You have to get outside. Admit it, indoors here or inside your head, you are a prison: get out and go for a walk.

the drop was sudden
precipitous all the way
down to the bottom
from there you can look around
flatter, closer to the ground

he made a picture
painted it all black, like tar
left chicken feathers
old bones sticking out of it
he took much consolation

from just making it
he had learned the mysteries
of Art, the anger
sometimes caught in it like traps
song thrushes stuck in birdlime

✧

#17

CARMODY: *I am an old man to be fooling around this way.*

BLIGHT: *Just think—if you don't make it back, no one will miss you.*

A Swede and a Norwegian were drinking *Akvavit* at a table in a bar. With each drink, the Swede would salute—"*Skål!*" Halfway through their second bottle, as they each tossed off the small cold swallow, the Swede called out "*Skål!*"—for the twentieth time. "Damn it!" the Norwegian cursed, and stood up. "Did you come here to drink, or to talk?"

not to make it
look any particular
way, but to do
such ordinary things
as the dance of poetry

put everything
you want into one box
you can shape it
to fit, shape anything
to go into the box

tell the story
of a girl in a car
in an orange grove…
wait! This is a family
poem, so just watch yourself

✧

#18

CARMODY: *I had another friend once, but suddenly he cooled, you know, stopped being my friend. Just like that.*

BLIGHT: *Never let anybody get too close.*

After driving all night to get to the shore, I went to sleep at the edge of a sand dune on the beach near Plymouth, Massachusetts. When I woke I was cold and covered with dew. The morning sea was calm and I saw half a dozen swans in the water-covered near-shore. I felt strangely vulnerable, that I had stumbled into a world where I did not belong.

it must have been
ironic (I almost said
iconic) when
you were dying all alone
all your victories sand

a cheerleader
she agreed to go with me
to the senior
prom if we could double date
with my football-hero friend

a town so safe
the kids could roam the streets
at all hours
making up stories, going
into empty buildings

✧

#19

CARMODY: *Your endless arguments exhaust me.*

BLIGHT: *I have just this to say…*

Trying to remember what was important is like grasping in the swash for something that flashed by—a silver fish, foam, or a jewel. Time sweeps over us in a rush, all at once it seems. Then it flows back, less of it and more slowly, carrying our memories, but depositing only a few of them at our feet.

he lay at night
eyes wide open, seeing
only the dark
and he tried to dream the things
he was always thinking

the two of us
being mutually useful
hurt each other
interpreting the pain
as train fare to the next stop

a loss of face
can be imaginary
and still ignite
bonfires of indignity
to immolate ourselves

✧

#20

CARMODY: *These identical redwoods side by side… sight along them and the parallels never meet, though you could trace them to the other side of the moon.*

BLIGHT: *Oh, God. Geometry lessons* dans le bois.

In the "Alabama Hills," in front of Mount Whitney in Inyo County, California, you can find relics from hundreds of movie sets, from old B-westerns with Tom Mix, Randolph Scott, and Hopalong Cassidy to film classics like *Gunga Din* and *High Sierra*. When I was a boy we had friends who lived in nearby Lone Pine, and we would explore the crazy rock formations there. Once, we stumbled upon the partly dilapidated set for a Saturday movie serial called *The Phantom*. We immediately fell into character.

adult frenzies
of psyche and alcohol
caught in the warp
of the poet's measured words
defined the modern age

I cannot read
what you say without thinking
I know better
erudite and pedantic
I can bleed all the life out

wild and forlorn
drops of light, high golden
sparkle and turn
where giddy with drumbeats
beat their old drum, drum, drum

✧

Ways of Transfiguration

CARMODY: *Well, I still say I've always done it this way!*

BLIGHT: *I've heard that before.*

We had imagined ourselves as somehow already French, although in truth we struggled to make sense of the language, had barely begun the endless paperwork required for a *Carte de Séjour*, and were only just beginning to think about the financial aspects of moving permanently to France. I see now that the whole idea was only a whim that grew out of our spending a few weeks in Provence during one sabbatical year. When you've rejected your last lifeline to the familiar, the totally new hangs heavily like wet flannel.

paper sheets crumpled
crease uniquely and gather
each in their own way
display identical laws
get out of each other's road

mash each smooth yellow
page down to a little ball
and then unfold it
do another and lay them
side by side. Check the wrinkles

was it simply all
that had happened, or should we
have seen a pattern
tracing its momentum in one
direction, catching the compass

On the small ranch my parents bought in California in 1943, there was a low barn (used mainly to house chickens) about twenty yards in length with a gradually sloping roof on either side. We put an old rabbit hutch off one end and we would then jump from the barn roof to the roof of the hutch, which would tip slowly over from the impact we made and deposit us gently on the ground. The farther away from the barn we put the hutch, the faster we had to run along the roof before leaping out into the air. There were untold calculations that had to be made at exactly the moment of takeoff.

what could the current
circumstance designate except
where we are and how
fast we are going? Each tick
of the second hand arrives

breathless, wondering
¿Qué Pasa? But Time's whirlwind
carries us backward
whatever new momentum
we might have gathered up

the future names all
that's going to happen, then
like the lizard's skin
it drops off and is promptly
replaced. What's the new skin called?

How we know, that history is never true, that history is just a story. Different from the banal passing of Time wherein simple living and dying, molecular processes, and the pealing and re-pealing of the bells, mark the passing; in history there's a literariness, drawn characters and poetically meaningful action. Logic and motive lift and sort whatever information is at hand and give it a form. Now, what the events properly historical have in common is that no one knows or has ever experienced them (whatever they are) exactly enough. They have always to be recovered and arranged by the art of historical writing; there are a million different stories about the past.

my grandmother told
fabulous stories making
them up as she went
you could learn what you wanted
from them. They never were true

if you only knew
what the excited molecules
in the wind desired
you might more skillfully explain
how they whistled in the grass

the reason we name
our past experiences
in the ways we do
is to let us symbolize
the whims of all our moments

#21

CARMODY: *It's a thick line between art and life.* [Pause] *In life you can say anything, go anywhere, do anything, or be anybody. The sky's the limit! But art, art is all about rules.*

BLIGHT: *Luckily, you don't have to name the thing until afterwards.*

Splitting the wood, piling it up, building a fire, lighting the kindling, pumping the bellows, and warming your hands. All of it can be expressed in the laws of Newtonian physics—weight, temperature, speed, and so on. But, what if we get closer up? How fast is this flame moving, the beautiful multi-colored dance of the fire? Look microscopically at the atoms and electrons, see how they pulsate, changing color at the "edge" of the flame—now here, then over there. It's all a matter of waves of possibility, the *quanta*. That same idea underpins the way they deploy outfielders to catch long fly balls without having to move at all—density of instance over time yields likelihood.

when someone dies
memory makes it hard
to realize
go into his empty room
you can't believe he's not there

his art of life
its deep consideration
melds proper form
into affection's trope
—to see one, find the other

the cherry trees
near Stockton droop low with fruit
like stone arcades
around deep green and red
cloisters shaded and cool

#22

CARMODY: *Please, don't just make up stuff. If you need something to say, try reflecting on our past together.*

BLIGHT: *What'll we do, then, about "once upon a time"?*

I remember being this particular person, the one I am now, since I was about 13, or so. Before that, my memories are more like those of an observer—whatever happened to that boy, me, happened as though he was in a movie. The interiority is missing. But, from 13, or so, up to (what is it now?) nearly 75, there is a continuous consciousness, one long single experience.

we killed a bird
remember that? with a gun
it seemed so small
then, when I held it up
hoping to feel triumphant

digging foxholes
with an army surplus
entrenching tool
holding off the Japanese
invasion of our meadow

like I'd swallowed
a brick, I used to say
a broken heart
feels heavy and sore like that
like you'd swallowed a brick

✧

#23

CARMODY: *They say you can't write poetry when you're making love!*

BLIGHT: [Puzzled.] *Did you never hear about the famous poet who was—"Pillow'd upon my fair love's ripening breast"?*[1]

A bad marriage can start to feel like a sickness; you wake to it in the morning, it's there over your shoulder all day long. You recognize the symptoms, but no one will reveal the causes to you and, certainly, no one mentions a cure. Everyone you know seems to want it to be fatal. But, if you're lucky, you meet someone. Not anyone you expected—she's too young, or she's a student and you're the professor, or, more likely, she's just someone you met in a bar. But the missing thing is there, the connection way below the surface, where your body meets her body, no questions asked. Maybe it works, maybe it doesn't, but you know this one clear thing: there's no going back.

a border guard
at the Trout River crossing
along Route 30
in New York, lusting to know
why she was so much younger

I was often
taken for the children's
grandfather
but I'd smile in the checkout
and say, "No, I'm their dad"

for thirty years
now, we've been on this date
my wife and I
passion, curiosity
sustained in equal measure

---

1. From "Bright star, would I were stedfast as thou art" (1820) by John Keats

✧

#24

CARMODY: *Ah, the light at the end of the tunnel.* [Pause.]
The darkness darkest just before dawn. [Stands.]
A stitch in time!

BLIGHT: *It could be that this, in fact, is a rehearsal for something bigger.*

I would get up every morning and resolve to make my thoughts more serene, but by midday I would be sloshing around in a swamp of tension, hostility, resentment, and self-pity. It was exhausting, really, and I did my best to hide it. I would smile, talk very nicely, and go out of my way to accommodate other people, but my problems remained on the inside; it was a circus in there.

in the autumn
when the leaves are yellow, red
the slightest breeze
reveals, of course, they're dead
and they fall like slow rain

what do we do
stuck in morning traffic
but theorize
what we might have become
predict the end of the world

I was afraid
to disappoint anyone
taking on work
I needn't have, neglecting
to sharpen my own skills

✧

#25

BLIGHT: *I think this is about as far as we dare go right now.*

CARMODY: *Coming up on it like this, you know, so suddenly—I was unprepared.*

BLIGHT: *I'll help you get through it.*

You are writing in long sentences, in eccentric phrases, and amidst connections so unlikely as to appear random; no—worse than random—whimsical, despotic. Then a word, *feels,* comes up, you look at it for a second, and then put it ahead nearer the start. Now what? The weave of language has been replaced by a wild wind that beats the branches arrhythmically against the roof. Who pretends to understand?

get up on it
and dance your little heart out
the man's coming
and he got his notebook out
he heard what you been doing

the worst of it
comes from mouthing the words
a sour sting
on your lips, teeth feeling rough
just saying it, the idea

feints the summer
breezes blowing; you step back
from the sentence
let the breath carry you
the rhythms running on

✧

#26

CARMODY: *We may have left them alone together too long.*

BLIGHT: *Without a go-between? Is that what you mean?*

When our neighbors were shipped off to Korea (he was an Air Force Captain), a gigantic moving van with U.S. Government plates pulled up in front of their house. A team of about 10 enlisted men got out, and removed electric saws, heavy scales, boxes of tools, and lumber from the van. Some of them began to construct large wooden crates. The others hauled furniture, clothing, pots and pans, lamps, trunks, etc. from the house. They wrapped everything, weighed it, and put it in crates, which were then nailed shut and hauled away.

separation
stretches focus and fringe
to the limit
paucity of stimuli
gives way to *Zerstreutheit*

wandering man
tucked behind his chariot
a complex life
hanging in plastic bags
culled from extravagance

behind the times
in long pathetic shadows
crawling their way
inside. Insect people
swarming over the wreckage

✧

#27

CARMODY: *There are no strangers on this street.* [Pauses to consider what he just said.] *To speak of.*

BLIGHT: *Home to the masses.*

In an installation entitled *Three Weeks in May (1977)*, Suzanne Lacy hung a map of the city in a mall near Los Angeles City Hall. The word RAPE was stenciled on the map wherever a woman was reported raped during the period of the show that lasted for three weeks beginning on Mother's Day, 1977. In an odd way, photographs of that map seem today almost like abstract art.[1]

you have to be
disturbed, only extreme
psychologies
deserve to be enshrined
in the structure of a poem

desperation
for a random woman
bottles of gin
senseless pain inflicted
arrogant in himself

look how cruelly
I can destroy myself
and anyone
close by. How else could I
be as special as I need?

---

1. For a video documenting *Three Weeks in May (1977)*, see artist's website (link retrieved on 15 August 2019):
http://www.suzannelacy.com/three-weeks-in-may

✧

Crépescule

CARMODY: *Dance halls of the Old West were centers of what might be considered fine art. There were no others.*

BLIGHT: *"Music has charms to sooth a savage breast, to soften rocks, or bend a knotted oak."*[1]

"Was it the Arnold?" the woman in large green overalls and a sheepskin was shouting out in the middle of 17th street, wrangling the traffic around her. "Or just the Edward, was it?" she yelled. "Or the Steven? Steven the Arnold… was that it?"

The Heineken guy was crossing the street with a hand truck of stacked beer cases; he was glad for her help slowing the traffic. Two early drinkers were locked in a loud argument about boxing or racism; it was hard to tell.

A police cruiser arrived in response to a fender-bender in the middle of the intersection of 17th and Capriccioso, where a City pickup truck had rear-ended a taxi. The cabby insisted they leave the cars exactly where they had come to rest until the accident report was filled out.

Then, it started to rain, soft and easy to begin with, but afterward torrentially. Everyone hurried out of the street; the woman in green overalls huddled under the maroon and white grocery awning and the beer guy put away the hand truck, dropped the canvas panels over the cases and kegs of beer in their rows, and drove off.

The storm darkened the street and neon signs reflected in puddles and where the collecting rainwater lay in sheets on the pavement. Convoys of autos crept by, wipers going, leaving a thin weave of tire tracks in the wet.

The stoplights at the nearest corner clicked through their red-green-yellow, and red-again phases, out of synchronicity with the lights at the farther corner. The weird rhythms of colored lights—click-clackety-click-clack—added musical syncopation to the scene.

The street-level door between Raymond's Shoe Shoppe and White's Bakery opened and a man in an artist's smock and black beret stepped out. He carried a large palette, the surface of which was rich in globules of brilliant oil paint, and a handful of brushes all maybe three feet long.

He walked straight into the street, pushed the bristles of a brush into a dollop of red and then into the yellow and with a wild, sweeping stroke upwards, he wiped a section of the sky into color, blocking out the rain. Then he dipped the brush into paint again, swept the sky again, and more of the sky turned red-yellow.

He put the end of a second brush into aqua-marine paint and then a little more yellow and some black. He swept the sky again and again, pushing the dazzling rainbow of colors higher up into the sky. He swept and dipped and swept and dipped until the cupola of the world was ablaze in color and the last bit of sun slid below the horizon.

---

1. From Act I of *The Mourning Bride*, a tragic drama in five acts by William Congreve (1670–1729), first presented in 1697

✧

#28

CARMODY: *My management principles do not include relations with employees.*

BLIGHT: *The long view, I presume.* [Pause.] *Look down there! It's the little people!*

CARMODY: [Hurrying over.] *Where?*

In 1947, in search of ever more interesting vacations, my parents bought a big canvas tent and we went camping in Ensenada, Baja California. It was, of course, wonderful to wake up every morning on the beach, to go swimming, cook our food outside, and all that. But, the most incredible thing of all was the Grunion run. Late one night, in the dark with only flashlights, we ran among a mass of small spawning fish that covered the sand all the way up to the high tide line. We were filling big pots with the squirming silver fish.

the octopus
preys on Dungeness crabs
at the bottom
of the aquarium
ruthlessly and brutal

we waded out
to our chests in the pond
casting poppers
into the nearly dark
listening for largemouth bass

seagulls cannot
apparently distinguish
natural food
clams, birds eggs, and dead fish
from garbage in the landfill

✧

#29

CARMODY: *I'm never anywhere I want to be.*

BLIGHT: *Because you're always right here.*

CARMODY: *I don't want to be here!*

BLIGHT: *Of course not. You can't "want" what's already so; it's not "missing."*

First, I went back East to attend college; in a month I was homesick and came home. Later, I moved to North Dakota, but that lasted only one summer. When I was twenty-five, I took a job in British Columbia, but I grew restless and blamed it on my colleagues, resigned, and moved away. It had always been a dream of mine to live in New Zealand, but I had been there less than a year when I found good reasons for leaving. Venturing forth, I always got cold feet—by the time I was forty, I was divorced.

like a stranger
eyeing unfamiliar
topography
harrowing rehearsals
of all the same old things

foreign airports
odors of local cuisine
habiliments
Ali Baba and his thieves
wild tales from Aleppo

I stopped to see
my old favorite teacher
the one who taught
me to love poetry
made me write a poem a day

✧

#30

CARMODY: *I am exactly like a helium balloon. I swell up or shrink down depending on the surrounding pressure.*

BLIGHT: [Indicating Carmody.] *Massive in the rarer atmosphere.* [Pause.] *Unable to descend, as it were, without disfigurement.*

As a part of our WWII games of soldiering, my brother and I would tie pieces of string to the corners of cloth squares cut from old bed sheets, and then tie the ends of the strings to large hex nuts. We would fold cloth, strings, and iron tightly and shoot it high in the air with a slingshot made from red rubber inner tubes. At its apogee, the parcel would unfold, the cloth fill with air, and the whole thing float slowly to the ground.

take everything
out that sounds concocted
what do her eyes
say? Such haughtiness is feigned
she's afraid she'll blow away

High Mass, "sung mass"
the Eucharist to music
brings the Bishop
to the parish, much pomp
and tips for the altar boys

long linear
gradient that his career
was following
before he blew himself up
refueling the lawnmower

✧

#31

CARMODY: *Perhaps only the ancient thinkers and writers could see into the tragedy of life.*

BLIGHT: *And into its absurdity.* [Pause.] *Altogether too many serious questions.*

CARMODY: *What about death?*

BLIGHT: *What about getting through this afternoon?*

Even as we got off the plane in Paris, you felt something was wrong. You know how Pissaro's *Boulevard Montmartre la nuit* seems so perfect? That was my idea of Paris. But, everywhere I saw and heard only crass commercialism, cars and trucks and buses, and American tourists. Right from the start the perfect Paris was set aside; we had to make do with something more like Harrisburg.

So what? I know
how lawless tongues incite us
reputations
suffer in the wake of
gossip. You're breaking my heart

instinct fails me
I am thrown under questions
against the grain
are you serious? Can you
go forward through the wreckage?

radical lust
often kindled poetry
of tender love
as well as frothing passions
sad, so sad, in their defeats

✧

#32

CARMODY: *We were laughing loudly all the way home in the car.*

BLIGHT: *I don't remember doing that.*

CARMODY: *Maybe you weren't there.*

In my dreams, when something bad happens to me it always feels well deserved. There is no specific sense that I've done anything wrong, just a sort of climate of guilt, so that I can never complain or try to explain. This makes for the sort of dream that you're very glad to awaken from, if you know what I mean.

in the doorway
living room lights behind him
my father, mad
switch in his hand, pauses
intensifying our fear

if the vacuum
broke and the power failed
that's exactly
what my wife will dream about
concrete things, and practical

anything can
operate as metaphor
for anything
else. Similarities
are not really required

✧

Part II

unrelenting
Time (what are the pneumatics
of its motion?)
tugs on my loosening skin
audible through the night

[…]

CARMODY: *I got right up on the stage, I did. And I danced with the Chorus, swung them around, stamped and spit. There was guilt enough for all.*

BLIGHT: *I was there. That was me on the tambourine!*

In the Groove

CARMODY: *Ah, the moment of inspiration! How long have I waited?* [Pause.] *Do you believe in inspiration?*

BLIGHT: *Breathe in, breathe out, breathe in, breathe out…*

At seventy-five you need either to ignore yourself altogether or bring in a roomful of machines and hook yourself up. Either you need to know precisely what's happening every minute or you just go along blissfully ignorant of the way your organs might be performing. You can choose deliberate and careful self-navigation or rely simply on flow, sort and count precisely all the coins in your purse (and then count them again) or race to catch up with the words that are writing themselves.

fixing the pipes
coiling wires and tubes around
vital organs—
bring the curtain up! Show them
theater out of the depths

things I cannot bring
myself to say out loud, I could
put in a poem—
backwards, of course, determined
to conceal *ictus* and *breve*

nothing of wars
now being waged savagely
had it not been
right in my kitchen listening
to the television news

✧

#33

CARMODY: "Into the alabasters/ And night blues," Wallace Stevens said.

BLIGHT: It's poetic sounding, I admit, but what does it mean?

CARMODY: [Patiently, to a fault.] *It was in reference to the "Barque of phosphor."*[1]

BLIGHT: [Overflowing irony.] *Oh well, that explains everything.*

It was 1955, somewhere in Wyoming, on the City of Los Angeles racing across the continent. I kept thinking how odd it was—there we were inside this warm, well-lit train, eating dinner, having a drink in the lounge car, reading a book in bed—all the time moving through the deep cold darkness outside. If you were out there in the dark, stopped in your car at a crossing, say, or awakened in your hotel room by the whistle, the world inside the train must have seemed tiny and mysterious, and if you imagined the people on the train looking out at you....

the steering wheel
from an old Ford sedan
fixed to a bike
an illusion of power
the center of attention

hot-air balloons
by the hundreds hissing low
over house tops
spill of a million colors
the smell of propane burners

I dreamt of flight
quixotic aeroplanes, under
telephone wires
over eucalyptus trees
in a painted landscape

---

1. "Barque of phosphor" and "Into the alabasters/ And night blues" are lines from a poem by Wallace Stevens, "Fabliau of Florida," in his first book, *Harmonium* (Knopf, 1923).

✧

#34

CARMODY: *Why are you standing there? What are you looking at?*

BLIGHT: *I was closely observing my world.*

An older man and a younger are standing on an ornate bridge over a shallow stream. The older gazes intently at the red and yellow leaves drifting slowly in the water. "Like Agamemnon's desultory Greeks," he says. Puzzled, the younger man notices that the sun creates leaf shadows moving on the creek bed. "Now, that's a poem," he says.

does the wind tease
Acacia limbs, or just push
and let them go?
no inanimate thing can
dance, mechanics forbids it

up close Chinese
opera's understated
passions hammered
out on a drum, captured
in many colored masks

did you notice
where the iron left marks
that indicate
he does his own laundry
is he fastidious, too?

✧

#35

CARMODY: *Just the littlest bit.*

BLIGHT: [Holding something in his open hand.] *This?*

Although in most cases nothing of this sort is admitted, I suspect that in the same way Rauschenberg famously erased de Kooning's drawing, so a lot of minimalist poetry is achieved by first writing out an ordinary poem (or stealing one, say, from John Ashbery) and then rubbing out words and sentences here and there. Accounts, as well, for the odd indents and spacing.

tanka are brief
by nature, a minimum
or maximum
five lines, counting syllables
"in and out like a cold bath"[1]

multiple short
love affairs only burn hot
they are over
before they go out! No time
to wait around for letters

they say that it's
diet that produced shorter
generations
see ancient suits of armor
old ladies at mass in Spain

---

1. Author's note: Friedrich Nietzsche, *The Gay Science*, §381

✧

#36

CARMODY: *I just love the look of the Objectivist line, don't you?*

BLIGHT: *"so much depends/ upon"*[1]

For the last three months there has been a huge renovation project going on next door. Every day, we've heard jackhammers and chain saws, the rumble of cement mixers, the oddly arrhythmic pounding of hammers, sawing, fitting, and shoveling. The noises started up early in the morning and only wound down in the late afternoon, six days a week. We've had only occasional brief glimpses of the crew through the bushes and snatches of spoken Spanish. Today, however, there was only one worker on the site; he was there to clean up.

sound, sense, and time
songs without formal music
just simple words
choosing the long vowel
makes something like a chord

expectations
of form, and the mind runs
ahead to wait
satisfaction even if
a little soporific

it's what you leave
out. Hard surfaces tell
the whole story
like clapping your hands to stir
up a cloud of butterflies

---

1. From "The Red Wheelbarrow" by William Carlos Williams, *The Collected Poems: Volume I, 1909-1939* (New Directions Publishing, 1938)

✧

#37

CARMODY: *Men were there, bearded and dirty, drinking cheap wine from bottles they passed around in brown paper bags.*

BLIGHT: *A pagan celebration, perhaps, or a refugee camp?*

Angry and curious students surrounded the patrol car that was meant to take away a political activist arrested for disobeying police orders. The car with its prisoner remained captive on the plaza for days, and radical speakers exhorted the crowd from its roof. Before climbing onto the captured police car to speak, Mario Savio and the other voices of the FSM took off their shoes and stood in their stocking feet.

four semesters
of lecturing, agony
on the Berkeley
campus; in my nightmares
I'm always late, and lost

east Africans
spread blankets on the street
selling *Mont Blanc*
knockoffs, *Prada* handbags
what are you willing to pay?

in Italy
prostitutes sit in beach chairs
side of the road
flirting with family men
quick connections in the car

✧

#38

CARMODY: *When you have counted out the syllables, sung them to the beat, and can feel the echoes fading slowly in your head, then you can talk to me about poetry.*

BLIGHT: *Sure, sure, but what about the story?*

In the 10th grade, Mr. Regalado, my English teacher, asked me out of nowhere what I thought of the Emily Dickinson poem with the words: "Past midnight, past the morning star!/ Past sunrise!" I replied, not much. "Maybe you think you could do better?" he asked. "Maybe," I said. Bring in poems, then, for the class, he ordered, one every day.

he wrote a poem
on a Turner morning mist
found the right words
for colors there and not there
light that comes from everywhere

I dreamed a kiss
from dear old Walt Whitman
a kiss so soft
it had no passion in it
no sex, pure camaraderie

they spray-painted
this morning powdery pink
stayed in the sky
until silver and gray
came on the wind from the sea

✧

Conundrum

CARMODY: *The great unknown!* [Pause.] *How do you react to that?*

BLIGHT: *To what, exactly?*

::

CARMODY: *I woke from a dream, but it persisted. In fact, I may still be dreaming.*

BLIGHT: *My worst nightmare!*

::

CARMODY: *I am not familiar with any Roman poets, nor the Attic graces. Here's a conundrum for us all—if we study well the past, will we improve the future?*

BLIGHT: *I don't know. How well did they do… back then?*

::

CARMODY: *Life's gamble: risking everything. You farm for a year, make sacrifices, and then bet it all on horse races at the annual fair.*

BLIGHT: *I stuck to the funnel cakes.*

✧

#40

CARMODY: *One thing I've learned, and I'll just say this much: you should never stick your nose into anyone else's business.*

BLIGHT: [Straightening up, belligerent.] *Are you trying to tell me what to do?*

When I resigned my appointment to the U.S. Coast Guard Academy in 1955, I had to stay on the post for another two weeks to get my way paid home to California. I continued to sleep in my quarters and ate my meals in the mess, but I was not required to wear a uniform, get up when the bugle played reveille through the loudspeaker, or salute anyone whatsoever. It was as if I were invisible.

tie and jacket
it is widely believed
will make children
better behaved, give them
a window on adulthood

an image is
merely illusion, some words
"an old oak tree"
nothing, if you've never seen
one, just your own if you have

a private poem
written in his head, recalled
in reflection
died when the author died
lingered between the lines

✧

#41

CARMODY: *The big picture, you know, like Whitman's "O span of youth! ever-push'd elasticity!/ O manhood, balanced, florid and full."*[1] [*Pause.*] *Does give you thought.*

BLIGHT: *What are you thinking about? Jesus!*

The first time I reached my hand into a girl's blouse, I did not know what I would find. I remember the smells, though, unfamiliar and intoxicating. Conversations with friends later made it all crude and vulgar, as when boys would talk to boys. All this was still a long way from love.

I worked with men
though I was only fourteen
I loved their talk
but recognized years later
they had always toned it down

love is easy
to fake, a gesture or two
can lead them on
but keep the reality
to yourself. Who needs to know?

being alone
the unchanging fundament
to put it clear
the world is there to drown out
the self's demanding clatter

---

1. From Section 45 of "Song of Myself" by Walt Whitman, in his book *Leaves of Grass* (1891–92 edition)

✧

#42

CARMODY: *What does it matter?* [Pause.] *We often hear that question.* [Pause.] *What does anything matter?*

BLIGHT: *Anymore, right?* [Worried.] *You meant—anymore.*

To get to the prison school you had to cross through the central rotunda, where the guards arbitrarily stopped and searched green-uniformed prisoners, who stood and waited in long lines on their way to eat, sleep, work, study, and daydream. The prisoners' eyes expressed nothing. They were forbidden to speak.

the dog's long chain
was clipped to a wire that ran
between two posts
as far as he could tell
he was free to wander

a real cowboy
one who needed open range
imagined cows
rumbling loudly through his dreams
put his hot brand to their hides

folding croissants
like pastry *scimitars*
from the Crusades
casts doubt on the Arab moon
nose against the glass

✧

#43

CARMODY: *Never joke about money.*

BLIGHT: *You ever hear of "funny money"?*

CARMODY: *Are you kidding?*

One night during a political thought class at the prison, there was a rush of footsteps and loud shouting down the corridor. A cluster of Corrections Officers ran by the classroom windows, batons at the ready; more shouting then, and a siren. My prisoner-students were out of their chairs and standing in front of the closed door. "Don't worry, Prof," Rashid, the Muslim Imam, said, "we got your back."

the *matinée*
was over, Bulldog Drummond
and Dick Tracy
followed us into the street
crime-stoppers up the alley

I heard Patti Smith
sing how the angel talked Johnny
up out of his grave
this was no time to give in
to the crazy dance of death

drunk with the crew
the night before the *France* sailed
from *Le Havre*—
a *gendarme* in shoulder cape
and *kepi* showed me home

✧

#44

CARMODY: *Do you think you could stand exactly here all night? I mean, wait right through the darkness for the sun to come up?*

BLIGHT: *Would you be there to talk to me?*

CARMODY: [Reflecting.] *I think we might manage that.*

BLIGHT: *I'm your man!*

We stopped at a hotel on an Indian reservation along the Trans-Canada highway in British Columbia. After dinner in the hotel, my wife and daughter went up to bed, and my brother and I crossed the road to a bar for a last beer. Earlier, the town had been pretty quiet, but now the bar and the parking lot were filled with clusters of drunken Indians. There were two RCMP moving among them, beating some with truncheons, and hurling insults at others. They were aided in this business by a man who appeared to be the white owner of the bar. My brother and I returned to the hotel, waked my wife and daughter, checked out right then, and left town. We drove all night through the mountains.

every quarter
hour the coal train runs through
Newcastle, Wyoming
from the Powder River pit
whistles blow all through the night

on vacation
trips my father would wake us
at three or four
with cocoa, and we'd drive
hour after hour in the dark

I kept vigil
wrapped in a towel on the beach
watching color
bleed back from the darkness
gray, white, blue, the golden clouds

#45

CARMODY: *Someone I used to know, that's all.* [Pause.] *Nobody, really.* [Pause.] *Why?*

BLIGHT: *I don't know. You just looked a certain way.*

She came to the end of the grocery aisle, and there he was. She shifted the baby securely on her hip. "Hey, how are you?" he asked. He almost reached toward the child. "Yours?" he asked. "Yes," she said. "Long time." "Yeah." "You happy?" he asked. "Yes," she said. "And you?" "Sort of," he said.

she painted stripes
ambiguous red ribbons
alongside blue
sometimes looks like a flag
or lead type in a job case

talked about poems
clever coinages of phrase
not exactly
wrong in the sense of false
but just barely feasible

lost from then on
couldn't keep his mind on work
just going through
the motions, dreaming of her
at night he danced by himself

✧

#46

CARMODY: *Tell me, how well did you know your father?*

BLIGHT: *My father was my hero.*

CARMODY: *Really?*

Instead of spending another summer at home killing time (I was fifteen), I got invited to travel halfway across the country and work as a lifeguard at my Uncle Warren's lake outside Sioux City, Iowa. In the middle of that summer, when he had to go to Tulsa on business, my uncle let me drive him in his 1953 white Cadillac limo, put me up in a hotel, and gave me pocket money. All the way there and back he taught me things—how to take a car through a long curve and how you can't spend the other guy's money.

oh, I don't know
time stretches so very thin
from every day
to once in a great while
it's harder to stay close

I see pieces
of his face in my mirror
especially
when I've grown a mustache
something surly round the eyes

a little brother
living with four big sisters
he always got his way
and was still using tantrums
when he was fifty years old

✧

#47

CARMODY: *You know, I don't feel a day older than—[Pause.]—forty? [Longer pause.] No, forty-five. That's it. No older than forty-five.*

BLIGHT: *But, how old are you, really?*

CARMODY: *Death's door, my boy, Death's door.*

Now, here's the thing. On my father's side the males tend to die in their sixties or early seventies. My dad died at 72, but he had two sisters who lived to be eighty. On my mother's side, there was a sister who died very young and my mother herself was dead by seventy. Another sister is now ninety, however, and her brother is in his late eighties. Here I sit, watching the quietus approach like the shadow of a building or a hill moving toward me as the sun goes down.

all winter long
he kept saying he'd be 40
his next birthday
fact is, he turned 39
and took the next year off

mixed-breed small dogs
live the longest, eighty
to a hundred
human years spent jumping up
on laps, licking faces

unrelenting
Time (what are the pneumatics
of its motion?)
tugs on my loosening skin
audible through the night

✧

Masters of Illusion

CARMODY: *I love plastic flowers, yellow orchids especially. They elude my deadly negligence.*

BLIGHT: *Against a painted forest mural background, scented aerosol, keep the AC low.*

In the past, I believe, life was simpler. There were fewer people, for starters, and the world was a good deal quieter. In such a setting, the individual's experiences had greater importance—what was seen, smelled, heard—than the indiscriminate buzz that surrounds us today. You can test this easily enough by trying to write a poem without letting any romantic claptrap about the past creep into it. Try to make something poetic out of the current, dirty push-and-shove, our dangerous looking characters, traffic noise, and the mad look in everyone's eyes.

rhythmic dull thumps
behind distant red flashes
feu d'artifice
French villagers remembering
German batteries near Reims

something went past
a curtain of sound and dust
I stood waving
as if watching a parade
the stragglers just walking by

on the way in
silky writing on the wall
shadow puppets
chatter, dance, and rage freely
my eyes give nothing away

✧

#48

CARMODY: *Oh, Vanity!*

BLIGHT: *Did you say something?*

CARMODY: *I am lamenting my own lack of recognition.*

BLIGHT: *You overlooked something?*

CARMODY: *[Pregnant pause.] I am being overlooked!*

Theoretically, each thing in the world is unique. No two Serra sculptures, no two Impressionist paintings, no two American poems, therefore, are exactly comparable, so how can we ever say that one is greater than another? In practice, the question of relative greatness (so necessary for commerce) is always resolved via the tautological cycle in which, having already determined some work that we prefer, we then stipulate that some particular trait that it just happens to exhibit is the *sine qua non* of artistic greatness.

I know this, why?
because X is always X
and never news
I ran to my brother's aid
even knowing he was wrong

on the outside
looking in, no place to be
the loser's perch
making sad excuses
for things that never go right

my favorite
things I always come back to
that's how I know
they're still my favorites
I wonder if they notice

✧

#49

CARMODY: *And then, bango! It was lights out! You know what I mean?*

BLIGHT: *And you never saw it coming?*

CARMODY: *Out of the blue.*

Stu Weschler was the student who most intimidated me in my first year of graduate school. He bragged, strutted, and lorded it over me, bludgeoning me with book titles and ideas I had never heard about. One day, in the Scope and Methods seminar, he presented a paper on Hegel. My heart sank; I didn't understand a word of it! As fate would have it, the professor turned to me and asked what I thought. "I couldn't make sense of it, " I finally admitted, crestfallen. "Nor could I," the professor said. Then, turning to Weschler, he added—venomously—"Just what was that supposed to be?"

in a poet's hands
a roll of quarters… waiting
scared, maybe drunk
he meant to bash someone
a terror out of the dark

the way earthquakes
come up the arroyo
softly rumbling
the house shakes like a child's toy
and then a sudden thud

I woke at night
sure it was a heart attack
a deep hard pain
right under my *sternum*
but it was my gall bladder

✧

#50

CARMODY: *Are you feeling any wiser now that we have gotten to the twilight years, so to speak?*

BLIGHT: *It seems to be getting darker, if anything.*

Crossing America in an old Honda, we always tried to get an early start on the day's flat driving. Usually, we would leave our motel at about 4:30 A.M., let the kids sleep in the back seat, and not stop for breakfast for three or four hours. The magical thing was to watch the night changing from dawn to morning twilight (our headlights and the streetlights still on) and, from there, to sunrise. I loved best that moment when the last tinge of darkness gives way to light and with the light—to color!

does red really
antagonize the bull
who sees only
yellow and blue (perhaps
waving the enemy's flag

I am standing
near the end, but on the cusp
would interfere
with the syntax's natural flow
throw the poem out, watch it glide

I am eager
for a new place to go
up the mountain
down the black hole. Pounding
syllables into place

✧

#51

CARMODY: *There is a moment when a work of art teeters on the brink.*

BLIGHT: *This is like the crisis in an old silent movie: the heroine, the train, the villain.*

CARMODY: *One step in the wrong direction....*

Words come from an interstice somewhere below consciousness. They come tumbling out, and magically assemble themselves in a form on the page. Faint fragments of music subtly nudge words together linking them—"cold alone, no fixed abode"—its *dum-te-dum-dum-te-te-dum* performs word-parthenogenesis, spewing the poem onto the page.

between hunter
and his game a silence
stretched to breaking
erupts across the wild fields
in a race of brain shadows

silken music
slides by itself in the wind
plays on our ears
wrapped loosely the lay of sounds
are these prescient melodies?

there is no wind
and these redwoods seem made
of green plaster
molecules at light speed
spread to my eye's rescue

✧

#52

CARMODY: *Here's the situation: our need to be loved is greater than our power to attract love.*

BLIGHT: *You could change your hair or buy a new dress.*

I sold my 1948 MG TC for about $2,000, which I then added to my savings to make the down payment on a small one-bedroom stucco fixer-upper in Victorville. I lived there rough while I refurbished things like plumbing, windows, and the roof. I sold the house then, and used my profits to finance a 2008 Peterbilt 387. So, that's how I came to be gazing up into a black sky thick with stars on Route 212 south of Laurel and Billings Montana.

unrequited
love along anodyne wires
he called last night
he was crying, so sad
she told him to stay away

you keep the child
in imagination's heart
especially
talking to the grownup
otherwise it's too tragic

we turn to things
their simple willingness
to satisfy
uneasy lusts themselves
demand nothing in return

✧

#53

CARMODY: *This is what we might call the scene of the crime. Notice how the natural impulses are blocked by built-in obstacles. Your bones dictate what you want, but ugly guards are there to strike you if you reveal anything about it.*

BLIGHT: *Is this not the scene of all crimes?*

how our parents
went about punishing us
O, Oedipus
"you always let me down"
they said, "where did I go wrong"

we justify
the violence of the state
ex post facto
standing dumbly aside
we let others speak for us

call your fancy
regrettable, sit on it
coming to terms
with rock, paper, and scissors
the wishes of my heart

✧

A Question of Murder

CARMODY: *I've always wondered if I could deliberately kill someone, you know?*

BLIGHT: *Say ten Our Fathers and ten Hail Marys.*

The new professor, teaching a class in politics at a maximum-security prison, was deadly curious about homicide. They were reading Machiavelli's *Prince* and talking about cruelty and the uses of murder, but the students seemed reluctant to talk. One of them, "Jaimey," a big Jamaican with dreadlocks, was squirming and grimacing in the back of the room. "Is something bothering you?" the new professor said.

"It ain't like that!" Jaimey said.

"What's not like what?"

"Killin'."

in the hermitic
quiet of his iron cell
the criminal sits
with his memories, all that's
left of what had been his life

The whole classroom went quiet, and the professor asked, "What's it like, then?" After a while, Jaimey said, "I was just looking to get high. One night me and my friend held up a grocery."

"This what you're in prison for?" the professor asked, but Jaimey ignored him. "I had a gun just to scare the guy. So, this grocer, an old Chinese guy, starts going crazy, banging his cane on the counter and we couldn't understand what he was saying. Then he comes after me with the cane and, I don't know, the gun sort of went off in my hand, all by itself. I saw his face explode and I ran out of there." He stopped talking and glanced around at the other inmates.

a reputation's
fragile built on such stories
and he could have said
he went in there with killin'
right in the front of his mind

"God, I was so sorry," he said. "I felt sick and I was scared. I kept running, but the pain wouldn't go away. So, I thought to myself maybe it was partly the Chinaman's own fault, you know. Why'd he have to carry on like that? Why didn't he just give me the money? So, now, I'm still running and I'm thinking he must have been crazy. And he came after me, didn't he? He couldn't just let it go, just give me the money, no, he had to raise hell. It was his fault, the selfish son-of-a-bitch! I was glad I killed him, shit, he had it coming."

we find out later
just why we did what we did
everything's confused
in the moment, heat and light
intermingling in action

"And that's where I was in terms of my thinking, you see, the bastard had it coming, and that's right when the police caught up with me. I was still hollering when they put me in the car."

the fever had cooled
his common sense recovered
its proper footing
life is lived now on two sides
of the wall, and in his mind

✧

#54

CARMODY: *Get inside the conventions and stay there. That's my motto. Just learn the rules and wear the mask. Or you could die trying something else.*

BLIGHT: *I like to be conventional most of the time, but then go berserk, like when I'm dancing.*

My experience of jealousy, fear, or anger as emotions always seems to come far short of the readily available and rich psychological accounts of what other people have felt. There is not only the vast clinical research, but also the accounts in novels, plays, and poetry. When I'm angry, even when I am totally outraged, it just seems flat and banal compared with the exquisite torments, for example, of one of Ken Kesey's psychiatric patients or Raskolnikov or Lady Macbeth.

medieval masques
dumb shows and a tap, tap, tap
a dancer whirls
mouthing his mad nothings
duc et dame sont pensif

we saw Brando
hollering up from the street
at painted flats
under the proscenium
back and forth on the lintel

the boy in front
of me in lecture snuffed
a cigarette
in my jacket pocket
I burned in helpless rage

✧

#55

CARMODY: *I know! I know how to do it!*

BLIGHT: *I just thought maybe you'd gone too far and needed help getting back.*

My father ate his supper off a TV tray and watched the Phil Silvers show. "Jews," he said, between bites, "it's always Jews." My mother said nothing. I said nothing. "Well," my father said, "am I right?" Later, in university, I discovered that I was small-minded about nearly everything. It took years of abuse and correction to alter my views. And, now, here I am in front of an audience of philosophers, about to present my paper, "Guilt and Mitigation in the Written Torah."

in the desert
three old men pool their wisdom
they're adding up
thoughtless opinions en masse
making an ersatz science

a few choice words
and a nod was all it took
to show me this
was not a liberal crowd
keep the class war to myself

learning to fit
in, you've muffled your Rs
broadened the E
and before you knew it
you were speaking New Zealand

✧

#56

CARMODY: *Imagine dinner for three in my apartment—my new lover, my wife, and I.*

BLIGHT: *Did your wife have to cook?*

The idea of equilibrium refers to the balancing of physical forces in a particular system, where we can define and measure those forces. Equilibrium in relations among people must always be metaphorical, however, the "forces" being conceptual generalizations about things like—how different people look; how they talk to one another; their strengths, movement, agility, intelligence, personal histories; how they reconcile the logical contradictions of religion, morality, and love. Do we measure these things in your inches, pounds, miles, journals, spans, or barleycorns?

mostly love songs
just something to talk about
balancing acts
where I stood out in the rain
I had nowhere to go

were you angry
the way I would have been
out in the cold
forced to stay in my place
unable to speak my mind

he was guessing
poet teaching us to poem
fundamentals
left aside sweet vagaries
that made his own poems famous

✧

#57

CARMODY: A rich man strolls by a poor man sitting in a ditch. Their eyes meet. Can you imagine it?

BLIGHT: [Recites.] ... *the history of all hitherto existing society is the history of class struggles.*[1]

Pat and I were just two little boys who once got into a fight on the school grounds. His family was rich, I guess you'd say, and mine was poor. His father arranged for him to work summers on a surveying crew in the mountains, while I picked boysenberries and assembled cardboard boxes in the packinghouse basement. Pat had his own bedroom with a private entrance; I shared a bedroom with my two brothers. He was given a new 1954 Chevrolet as a present. I saved up $300 and bought an old Plymouth sedan. Pat eventually went to Stanford and I went to the State College. And so on.

why not permits
for beggars on public streets
sealed in plastic
like driving licenses
worn on chains round their necks

money for love
drop your nickel on the drum
get your kisses
they say this is the world's
oldest affection machine

what can kill you
does not make you stronger
jump from a bridge
in making a statement
you've just cut yourself off

---

1. From *The Communist Manifesto* (1848) by Karl Marx and Friedrich Engels

✧

#58

CARMODY: *Locale is everything. You can take off all your clothes at the gym, but not in the aisles at the supermarket.*

BLIGHT: *The Seraphim in their hot raiment, the cool Cherubim.*

We were walking through the eroded trenches of the WWI Beaumont Hamel battlefield. We passed what had been the Newfoundland Regiment's line and were looking back from where the Germans had looked down—such a short distance, all smooth, curved, and rounded now, and carpeted quietly with grass. In a gardener's compost pile I found the rusted-off top of a German barbed-wire post, a sharp point ahead of an iron curlicue loop, like a lower case cursive "e."

he spent, postwar
a year or two in France
studying art
though the smell of battle still
lingered in the *bocage*

on roller skates
girls like birds trapped indoors, dart
the *Carrefour*
locating *haricots verts*
scope the *charcuterie* mile

war medals pinned
above his left breast pocket
he crossed the street
shook our hands in thanks he said
to America

✧

#59

CARMODY: *I'm right on the verge of saying something political—I'm that fed up!*

BLIGHT: *The art of the possible…*

When I was an undergraduate, I first majored in "pre-professional life sciences," what my father called "pre-med." I meant to honor his wish that I become a doctor. Later, I switched to English, but never could find my way there; the professors were so delicate in their tastes, so subtle. I finally became a Political Science major, and I was there the day Professor Charles Hickman Titus declared: "Politics is the art of getting what you want and making people like it."

it isn't fair
a man concerned with outcomes
died the year he
retired; his weakened wings
couldn't keep him off the ground

what if power
dared to count iambic feet
to authorize
a public music, sing-song
here's the way a poem should be

domination
sung in unrhymed couplets
sovereignty's muse
policing public speech
metaphors in common things

✧

Substitute

CARMODY: *Creating a metaphor is easy. You think about something you want to capture, like love, say, or the destruction of your dreams. Then, you find something to talk about that will substitute for love, for destruction. It doesn't matter what it is, either; the farther away, the better.*

BLIGHT: *When you die, it's just like they turned off the lights.* [Pause.] *Are you there?* [Pause.] *Hello? Hello?*

✧

#60

CARMODY: *Swift the river, swiftly towards the sea.* [Pause.] *Does that sound like it's too late to turn back?*

BLIGHT: *"...nor all your piety nor wit..."*[1]

As kids in Riverside, California, we used to swim in the cold water of the Gage Canal as it wandered through the orange groves or was terraced on a brown hillside. You could float on an inner tube for miles, but you had to be careful about the grates where the water went under a road or into a mountain. My mother made me promise I would never go in the canal again after a child's bloated body was pulled from one of the grated entrances.

on the last day
of my life, the last day
sunup, never
to be seen again, sadder
than impending sundown

as yet unseen
tendering its obscured hope—
Oh, I can wait!
the memories I'll have
red and dampened crépuscule...

it's at the end
how short the journey seems
we'd just begun
I'm scratching around now
for meanings I might have dropped

---

1. From *The Rubaiyat of Omar Khayyam* (LXXI) as translated by Edward Marlborough FitzGerald

✧

#61

CARMODY: *No more! I am finished.*

BLIGHT: [Looking left and right.] *Lights.* [Pause.] *Shut her down. It's a wrap!*

You know you are growing old, first, by things you pick out from other people's reactions and, second, by your own internal monitoring of increasing weakness, difficulty, and slowness. There have been times when I was just walking along, thinking of somewhere I wanted to go or something I planned to write down as soon as I got home, and then I would pass a store window or a mirror and see myself—shorter, more wrinkled, grayer, and more…more (oh, I don't know)…caved in?

you barely hear
each day as it unrolls
with a soft swooshing
it starts, with the sun up
nothing at all at the end

how much longer
can this singular line stretch
that reaches back
from here, where the years pile up
to that invisible boy

the game's last play
the last smoke in the pack
the bottom swig
just move now toward the door
with a wave of your hand

✧

#62

CARMODY: *I dreamed about playing in a band, you know. I'm up there with my guitar making fabulous moves.* [Pause.] *I'm singing it out like it is!*

BLIGHT: *And I come in with this beautiful woman on my arm and I light a cigar with a twenty-dollar bill and I send you up a bottle of iced champagne. We nod to each other.*

A couple of memories driving or flying over parts of the country, a book or two that you've read, the raster images stored in your brain from hours watching television, the music, the flag, the words—these are the sum total of your being an American, a New Zealander, French, or whatever. The reality—the physical things that make up a country—is beyond anyone's direct grasp. We know who we are—abstractly in our imaginations.

I can see trees
blowing wildly in the storm
with my eyes closed
I hear songs never written
a zephyr kisses my cheek

the grass was burned
along the Mason-Dixon
line nearby trees
black, leafless, and no longer
marking pathways to the South

why ask for more
the processes of thought are
mysterious
you wake up suddenly
were you lost in reverie

✧

#63

CARMODY: *Abracadabra!* [A sweeping gesture. Pause. Nothing.]

BLIGHT: *You're never satisfied, are you?*

He came back from a round of golf looking awful—pale and frightened. He left his clubs in the car, came in the house, lay down on the couch, and said, "I think I've had a heart attack."

if you betray
these things you say you stood for
and don't get caught
you're tempted to imagine
there'll be no consequence

I begged for one
last kiss, but she closed the door
permanently
I turned away thinking now
I was more than ever lost

not everyone
dreams in color, in such depth
less images
I think, than ideas of
people, things loudly spoken

✧

Psychotherapeutics

CARMODY : [As Othello] *There was in my ear a grave imbalance sent me lurching out of bed, stumbling in the grass.*

BLIGHT: [As Iago] *You are perhaps too finely tuned to self.*

He was always asking whether this or that could make you cry, whether it ever made you cry, and what was wrong with that?

turning things around
he studied symptoms just the way

He was building up a character that he could play out on the street, for his inward peace or when coping with others.

you might learn your lines

So, he researched the lineaments of noble personae; the courageous chin and strength linked to sensitivity.

had you been cast in some sad
theatrical tragedy

He believed if he could only find the tendrilled way down to his true thoughts, he might verify the workings of his mind.

how they might admire
his style if they could understand

So everyone might see not just his actions, but the deeds illuminated by a script, a sort of dictionary of his morals.

see something deeper

The courageous touches then applied—a walk, of course, a subtly halting speech for emphasis, his heart worn on his sleeve.

how he quivered when pained
his anguish so exquisite

Part III

senses deranged
the soft connection between
actions and words
dissolves; your words are scattered
to fall to the ground in poems

[…]

CARMODY: *You have to get their attention. Whatever gets their attention...*

BLIGHT: [Strikes a pose.] *I labored for years alloying thespians with pedagogues.*

L'Art de la guerre

CARMODY: *How could you possibly translate the horror of war into music?*

BLIGHT: *War in the political calculus?* [Pause.] *Everyone up and march around the hall!*

When I was a Cadet at the U.S. Coast Guard Academy, my favorite thing was close-order drill with M1 Garands on Saturday mornings. It moved like a dance to me; under the brusque eccentric commands—"column left," "by the right flank," "to the rear," "right oblique," "Order…Arms!" But, the drill's origins are not in the dance—this parading is a remnant of the historical methods by which troops in tight battle formation and under fire maneuvered to face the enemy, to shift the concentration of force, to open the line for volley fire, to form square, to advance over the bodies of the fallen. It's as old as Philip of Macedon.

a Christian boy
he was sent twice to Iraq
later offered
the chance to skip a third tour
working as a recruiter

when we played war
in the fields behind our house
we made *da-ta-da*
musical sound effects
charging into the jaws of death

Machiavelli
was unable to drill troops
though he had written
Dell'arte della guerra
around a fantasy battle

✧

Stereotypicals

CARMODY: *But, doesn't it have to make sense?*

BLIGHT: *It makes sense to me!*

At first the sunlight could hardly reach us through the miles of interlaced and leafless forest branches.

where the river bends
outside currents abrade the bank

But later, we could separate willow withes from maple boughs and thin oaken twigs deeply in the woods.

there the flood comes through

Imagine, then, a stickle world turned to browns—darkest in the forest shadows, palest on the faded fence.

while slower inside vectors
build and push the river out

✧

#64

CARMODY: *What do they get out of just mixing words up? I mean, when they write something like—"there fell a fish one time out of a lake so wet."*

BLIGHT: *Well, it sure makes me read more carefully.*

Let's go to the flea market tomorrow. I'm looking for one of those mannequins that dressmakers use, an aluminum potted palm that no one ever has to water, a string of really old-fashioned Christmas lights, and a Lazy Susan. There's a stall at the far end where they sell jewelry made entirely from antique clock movements—Seth Thomas, Hermle, Gustav Becker, Badische, Ansonia.

cryptic drawings
seen in the table's troughed oak
meadows, a woods
hedges where the wind parts
the branches, a grassy brook

pewter candles
on the plate shelf, never lit
hold memories
is all, alike old bottles
faded bills on a spindle

in a side lot
rest a dozen rusty cars
among the weeds
like chapters in the story
of these people, the last ones

✧

#65

CARMODY: *Listen! Listen! After each roar of the waves, there's a hissing, sucking sound. And look! The sand actually moves, all of it at once.*

BLIGHT: *"And then went down to the ship,*
Set keel to breakers, forth on the godly sea..."[1]

My grandfather was a blacksmith with a shop in the small Iowa farm town of Moville. When he died, my father rented a trailer and hauled most of the blacksmith and farrier equipment to California and installed it all in our garage. There were lathes and big drill presses, an acetylene welder, a band saw, grinders, pincers, rasps, and a huge hoist that hung from the roof beams for pulling engine blocks. Oh, I can't remember it all. One by one my father taught himself to use them.

old oiled oarlocks
alongside M1 Garands
brass field glasses
and a gas mask from Belgium
the faint smell of gunpowder

just looking through
discarded cups and saucers
who is to say
how any of this end game
should be interpreted

as we exit
some last vibrations of our
speech continues
to be heard by the subtle
ear, faster than memory

---

1. Opening lines of "Canto I" [1922] by Ezra Pound, *The Cantos of Ezra Pound* (New Directions Publishing, 1996)

#66

CARMODY: *I want to talk about each and every little thing that happens before they're sorted into important and not so important. The raw stuff, you know?*

BLIGHT: *One-way ticket, yeah!*

I woke around 3:00 AM on the couch in a strange living room to loud crashing and banging. Someone I thought I remembered from the party was still up and drunk. He had taken a log from the unlit fireplace and was walking around the room smashing furniture with it. He was talking very loud to some woman who obviously was not there. He decided not to hit me and, instead, told me about the married woman he was in love with and who wouldn't talk to him on the phone. I said I'd drive him over to her place; that would get him out of the house, I thought. On the way, he insisted on stopping to call her from a pay phone, and when he was trying to fit the coins into the slots, I drove away.

a pair of crows
high up circle the canyon
we saw the one
a long thin stick in its beak
turn and fly behind the trees

words can rattle
and ricochet off the walls
sourced in madness
they appeal to the troubled
and are made into anthems

undiscounted
each wild pandemonium
could be the poet's
own prancing murderers, ghosts
demented kings and donkeys

✧

Talking to Myself

CARMODY: *My father told me, "Just do what you want. I don't care."*

BLIGHT: *Right, and after that you became a slave to your passions.*

::

CARMODY: *I woke up from my nap today and for a second or two I didn't know who I was.*

BLIGHT: *A little whiskey does the same for me.*

::

CARMODY: *Do you remember when you first became aware of your own personal identity?*

BLIGHT: *You mean, the first time I talked to myself?*

::

CARMODY: *Have you looked to see if there's another way out?*

BLIGHT: *We came in together, and that's the way we'll leave.*

::

CARMODY: *How far up the road can we push this wagon? I mean, if we never run out of energy.*

BLIGHT: *Never? [Pause.] Forever.*

✧

#67

CARMODY: *The rhetorical fervor rises and falls on its own within me. I'm never sure what mood I'll be in.*

BLIGHT: *I am like blank sheet-music pages. Not noted as yet.*

He was sitting on a window ledge in the departure lounge, his right leg angled over his left, writing in a small brown leather notebook. A novelist, I thought, or a poet. He was oblivious to the stream of travelers that parted to go around him. He wrote carefully with a Mont Blanc fountain pen, pausing every couple of words to consider what he had just written. I walked behind him and looked over his shoulder. The page was covered with doodles—Ionic curlicues, assorted spearheads, elaborate compass roses, labyrinths, mazes, and crosses of every kind.

some hours go on
for days when you are really
thinking in them
and not just feeling good
looking first this way, then that

my grandfather
punched stemmed roses into brass
shell casings
with a French point-peen hammer
in lulls between barrages

teams of students
and concrete finishers built
the block letter
C on the side of Box Springs
Mountain—pure metonymy

✧

#68

CARMODY: *The trouble with making plans, of course, is the future. There is no future, as such; I mean, there's nothing in the future, right now.*

BLIGHT: *"What we can't say we can't say, and we can't whistle it either."*[1]

kids in school
mouthing the words of anthems
punch each other
under the table, giggle
watching ramparts glaring red

if tomorrow
happens to be like today
what can we say
about the differences?
call them all—yesterday

no abstractions
can reach deeply enough
into our thoughts
they just stay on surfaces
like color or smoothness

---

1. Frank P. Ramsey (1903–1930), quoted in *F. P. Ramsey: Philosophical Papers*, edited by D. H. Mellor (Cambridge: Cambridge University Press, 1990), page 146

✧

Richard Diebenkorn:
Three Ekprastic Moments

Preface

CARMODY: *The painter spoke long before; he's over and done with.*

BLIGHT: *Would he mind, do you suppose, if I tried to lure the music out?*

the eye remembers
till it looks away, the details
unfixed, nameless, small

I can see the presence there, the viewer's dark silhouette and the brightly colored painting;

where the yellow bar, lying
across the top weighs down

the distance thick with looking, the canvas, wholly muted, strains against the air;

a man's afraid to look
away and tries to pound at least
the blue into his dreams

if he could walk in, go right through the surface of blue and yellow paint, he'd find it.

the air is tense, leaden
the moment justly frozen

Ocean Park #116 (1979)[1]

CARMODY: *Let me take a stab at this one. I'll tell you what I think he was up to.*

BLIGHT: *A tapestry... and maybe an airfield.. and... did you see, the top, the curve partly erased?*

call this the "Blue One"
a fallen patch of sky, but not

If he made six good original lines with a ruler he could have divided up the whole canvas.

really. On inspection

In desperation he would have matched this with that to reach up into the two-toned yellow bar.

a blue wash spread over lines
delineating nothing now

Like a bird calling faintly across the lake at crepuscule; you're wondering if you really heard it.

if you were to try
to describe Van Gogh's Starry Night

This picture is a composition of geometric shapes, a student's notebook, filled with erasures.

brush stroke by brush stroke

When your thoughts are determined to find the subject, the sky or the town, they stop and surrender.

*and could not take refuge in
the idea of a tree or stone*

Just lines, angles, colors, textures, and frustration, over and over.

*two lines of order
at the stop, the first things drawn*

You can see readily each rectangular form is different from the others, like ears or noses would be in portraiture, or leaves on a tree.

*obliterated
radius of a circle*

The lines and boxes, the colors alternating make a visible metaphysics, an ontology of whimsy.

the large fields watery, opaque

Ocean Park #118 (1980)[2]

CARMODY: Each one is really different, of course, but they're also just the same.

BLIGHT: The same notes can be played in a lot of different ways.

you wouldn't describe
the shapes of all the letters
interpreting a poem

If I say there's an orange and black needle entering top left, splitting the picture like a wedge

you have to enter behind
the surface marks, go deeper

between the brightly layered bands at the top and ever larger polygons in pale colors

for all the balancing
none of this means anything
not the light, not joy

a faded purple belt with black lines fits under it and then mistakes just showing through.

you might imagine your way
through to his true state of mind

1. *Ocean Park #116* (oil and charcoal on canvas, 82"x72"; 1979) by Richard Diebenkorn (1922–1993) is held at the Fine Arts Museums of San Francisco and may be viewed at The Diebenkorn Foundation's website: https://collection.diebenkorn.org/objects/550/ocean-park-116?ctx=5fd4feed-f9fa-48e8-be20-f96b259223a1&idx=1

2. Diebenkorn's *Ocean Park #118* (oil and charcoal on canvas, 93"x81"; 1980) may be viewed at The Diebenkorn Foundation's website: https://collection.diebenkorn.org/objects/552/ocean-park-118?ctx=316ba5f9-5049-449c-9415-ee0b50609ab4&idx=0

Neither work is reproduced herein, given The Diebenkorn Foundation's quality-assurance restrictions regarding print-on-demand books.

However, both paintings and numerous others by the artist can also be viewed in "Richard Diebenkorn's Ocean Park Series," posted by Poul Webb on 15 February 2011 to his blog, *Art & Artists*:
http://poulwebb.blogspot.com/2011/02/richard-diebenkorn-ocean-park-series.html

See also *The Drawings of Richard Diebenkorn* by John Elderfield (Museum of Modern Art, New York; Houston Fine Art Press, 1988):
https://www.moma.org/documents/moma_catalogue_2140_300062884.pdf

✧

#69

CARMODY: [Gesturing with his arms, making large circles.]
None of my questions have answers. I can't understand it.

BLIGHT: *I dreamed last night that Chinese fans of glittering red—*

CARMODY: *I don't want to hear it.*

I went to Professor Carney's office after class to ask a question about the Puritans. As I entered his office, he turned to me and said: "I just had a physical and the doctor told me I had the youngest body he's ever seen in a forty-year-old man!" He stuffed *Balkan Sobranie* into his new GBD, lit it, tamped it down, and lit it again. "What's on your mind?" he asked.

"Jonathan Edwards," I said.

"What about him?"

"Lecture XV," I said, and then I read out: "The wrath of God burns against them, their damnation does not slumber; the pit is prepared, the fire is made ready, the furnace is now hot, ready to receive them; the flames do now rage and glow. The glittering sword is whet, and held over them, and the pit hath opened its mouth under them."[1]

The professor listened, and was quiet for a moment. "Congress shall make no law," he recited, taking his pipe out of his mouth for a second, "respecting an establishment of religion, or prohibiting the free exercise thereof."[2]

books left open
on the reading room table
lights going out
you can feel the rage cooling
disputations calming down

monks came to school
wearing gray hooded tunics
for renascence
children of seven or eight
searching their dark consciences

looking beyond
the ordinary world for
enlightenment
wave after wave, a muttering
sea of words, words, words

---

1. From the sermon "Sinners in the Hands of an Angry God," delivered by theologian Jonathan Edwards on 8 July 1741

2. Establishment Clause of the First Amendment (15 December 1791) of the Bill of Rights in the *United States Constitution*

#70

CARMODY: *It presses on a nerve whenever I bite down like this.* [Clenches his teeth, tenses his jaw.] *Oh… Ow!* [Pause.] *You see what I mean?*

BLIGHT: *Another miscarriage of justice.*

Two shadowed roads lead through inland orange groves down to the river. They separate there, one road crossing the river by the old brick bridge and the other turning immediately to travel along the nearer bank. The road on the other side, called appropriately, "Bridge Road," turns into a levee-towpath on the opposite higher bank; the near side follows the river loosely, moving away here and there to connect with the odd village, but it always comes back; it is called the "River Road." The two roads arise from a powerful metaphor.

each villager
grows potatoes, onions
and carrots, buys
bread to eat with the soup
homemade wine in demijohns

the bus leaves off
tourists near a cluster
of Quonset huts
where local arts and crafts
are sold. Captive audience

night can be black
far away from the town lights
obsidian
invisible skies lit up
by a trillion, trillion stars

✧

#71

CARMODY: *Sometimes I feel so dejected; the meaning of life eludes me.* [Pause.] *Perhaps, there is no meaning.*

BLIGHT: *Questions, questions...*

Professor Zinna said once that anything can be a metaphor for anything else. "Just pick something," he said. "Take this chalk, for instance." He hesitated, and then asked—"Instance of what?" Of course, I thought immediately of how you "chalk one up," then about someone giving a "chalk talk, and there's the tailor's chalk and chalk in gesso." Chalk could stand for school, for all kinds of writing, for authority, etc. "Charles VIII conquered Florence with only his quartermaster's chalk," Professor Zinna said, "as Machiavelli wrote in Chapter XII of *Il principe*. Chalk on your hands, broken pieces of chalk, a chalky taste... you take it from there."

fell short again
where is my multi-colored
quadrilateral
my lines of pale perfection
my glued-up eagle feathers?

on the sidewalk
places where you could fall
to the center
of the earth or fly straight up
to heaven, up to heaven

this little stick
that I picked up on the way
symbolizes
the weapons of modern war
the growth of community

✧

Le verbe être

CARMODY: *If we moved to a surreal town, one with feathers and a horn, some of us would get noticed, that's for sure. [Pause.] Agnes, there, with her litter of aphorisms, would be a good candidate.*

BLIGHT: *Write me a sentence that reveals a truth about the world.*

He was insane; everyone said so. He would just be standing on the sidewalk and suddenly he'd start jerking around, wave his arms, and throw his head this way and that. So, against every rule there is, I walked over and asked him what was wrong. "It won't stop, man," he said. "What?" I asked. "The sounds," he yelled. "They never go away. They just pile up and get louder and louder. Hear that bus? Jesus! Listen to that bus. And now it's added to yesterday's buses, all of them, all of the noise all piled up." I stared at him. "Oh my God!" he roared. "Another bird. Listen to them! There's a billon damn birds out there!"

so, listen here
there's a poetry of life
doesn't measure
everything in dollars or
years, stakes something on the heart

you have to know
something the hard way sometimes
to remember
what goes with what, what doesn't
convulse far constellations

you cannot draw
the line between words and things
with a piece of chalk
most of the time just babbling
where stick connects with just—stick

✧

#72

CARMODY: *Give your life a name then, and go on your porch and call it out, like you were calling a child or dog that had wandered off.*

BLIGHT: [Puts his fingers in his mouth and whistles loudly.] *Whee-oooh-wheet!*

Over and over, with a humorous touch, he would abandon the search for inner meaning and then later go back to it. But, no matter how deeply he would learn to penetrate his own thoughts, only the hollow echoes of old questions came back to him. He would sing, then, popular love songs and songs about cowboys or bartenders. There was never anything below the glassy surfaces; only the red lay underneath.

he looks, he sees
there's nothing in the mirror
turning inward
the unimportant things
all in reverse, left for right

what is not here
was never and your searching
won't bring it here
start out with an empty bowl
learn the necessary shapes

just as voices
in the distance faded, mute
in lonely woods
frighten us more than the snarl
from a wolf closer up

✧

#73

CARMODY: *At the end of the whole thing I haven't even one friend. I had all that need and found no nourishment.* [Pause.] *What would you call me?*

BLIGHT: *Irresistible? A cab?*

The imaginary intimacies of politics, the countenanced ravaging of the masses, the furtive ways we search for escape routes, for paths out of ourselves; is it love we feel for billboards and bumper stickers? Study the faces on television—the earnest reporters, the enraged opposition, the cheap makeup on our leaders, telltale lipstick showing through when they come before the camera, the fatigue and boredom behind the podiums. We ought to feel much dirtier than we do.

she always talked
as if someone far away
and likely dead
was the interlocutor
one who really had her ear

then hard music
a symphony on one horn
broke into me
ground its rough boots in the glass
that lay shattered all around

why would I think
the effect that anything
might have on me
mattered at all? What if I
roamed the streets, saying, "See? See?"

✧

#74

CARMODY: *Something so beautiful it was frightening? How sentimental.*

BLIGHT: *Try looking down into the Jeffrey asbestos quarry in Quebec sometime.*

CARMODY: *Big, huh?*

BLIGHT: *Takes your breath away.*

Viewed from the bluff, the coal train from Powder River stretches all the way to the horizon. Fifty-one Burlington Northern coal trains a day through Newcastle, Wyoming; day and night the diesel horns sound at three crossings. Trains, as long as 120 to 150 open side-loading coal cars, lose three percent of their load in the air on the long trip to power plants in Georgia. Engines in the front and at the rear pull and push while railroad buffs all along the highway in Wyoming make videos of the endless flow of coal.

dirt on your hands
you scrape away the details
looking beneath
for something lovelier
no beauty in black iron

the air in Christchurch
New Zealand was black with coke
smoke from stove fires
in kitchens all over town
—your nose filled up with it

native peoples
dance and speak oddly wordless
incantations
to redeem the continent
take back the rivers and the trout

#75

CARMODY: *All the words connected loosely, apples called upon to feign, furtive and complacently, to innocently* sprach *un-goodness.*

BLIGHT: *Is there something under there? Let me see!*

And, then, my father would fly into a rage over nothing at all—too much salt, too little sugar for his taste. But, it would not be an authentic rage. It was patterned on something he'd seen in a movie or read in a book. The annoyance to start was a pretext to get him started, but the structure of the thing, the exaggerated gestures, the curses and threats, was scripted according to whatever model of an emotion he was displaying. The same was true for moments of passive acceptance or self-pity or even grief. You could never believe a word he was saying in moments like that.

the word of God
he gave freely, spoke it quick
like lightning
lit the place up all at once
then left us in the dark

les tropisms
geologic leafless trees
growing downwards
metaphorically before
eyes in the back of our heads

out of my mind
here at the end of my wits
before my time
fishing with string and a hook
in a river of guile

✧

By Their Fruits

CARMODY: *I have been looking all my life for someone who would tip me up straight and point me in the right direction.*

BLIGHT: *"Ye shall know them by their fruits."*[1]

When the police arrived, the old woman was still in a state of confusion, having stumbled over the row of decorative bricks by the bay window and rolled down the slopping lawn to the road. She declined any kind of medical attention, though, and would have walked off to town in a sort of huff, if the police had not insisted on a medical examination.

"I just want you to know that I've seen what's going on around here," the old woman said, turning her face away from the policeman.

The young Trooper winked at us, put her in the back seat of his cruiser, and drove away.

"She actually seemed annoyed with us," Betsy said, "and she was the one trespassing."

"Does anyone know who she is?" I asked, as we watched the police car turn at the big hedges, and disappear.

"I think we should check if she did find anything," Betsy said. I agreed, because I had seen the woman trying to look in the dining room windows just before she tripped.

"I doubt she was ever inside the house," Laura said.

"Anyone see her before she fell"? Betsy asked. "I mean before Bob saw her looking in the windows?"

"I've seen her in the village," I said. "At least I think so."

"Maybe she used to own the place," Laura speculated.

"Or maybe she escaped from the State Hospital," Betsy said, and rolled her eyes. "You never know."

"I'm going to ask around about her in town tomorrow," I said. "This place could have been an old commune, you know?"

"And what if she used to live here," Betsy said, "and she's got a stash of her own buried here and she was coming back to dig it up?"

"Jesus Christ," Laura said.

"She might have a fortune in drugs stashed around here," Betsy said.

"Maybe the house used to actually be part of the revolution," I said, and everybody laughed.

"I think we all need a drink, Betsy said.

"Be careful over there by the bricks," Laura said. "It's a long way down to the bottom."

---

1. Matthew 7:16 from the Sermon on the Mount in the New Testament of the Bible (King James version)

✧

From the Doctor's Rough Drafts

CARMODY: *I sometimes feel I am not close enough to my fellow man, you know, I feel alone, maybe even unloved.*

BLIGHT: *I've never been much of a joiner, myself.*

In the course of wondering just who I was, I felt a strange pull and push as I thought for a time I was at one with everyone else, a cell in tissue, an atom in the iron; but then I immediately saw myself as a peregrine circling alone in the sky, a hunter, just me against the world. I looked down at the ground, then, into the field where a falconer stood holding out his thick-gloved arm beckoning to me and I felt duty like a weight slow my wings, shorten my sailing circles, and gradually draw me down to the field and the waiting ornate leather hood.

voices on the wind
thin shrill voices breaking up
far in the distance
I was dreaming of flying
setting my course for the clouds

as if in a song
each thing was an instrument
the cobblestones sang
in a kind of choir, each
leaf tapped out its own tempo

amidst confusion
our ear makes separate sounds
distinct in the noise
we pick out songs from thunder
tap, tap tapping with the rain

✦

In the Garden of Delights

CARMODY: *Everyone wants to pick up and go live at the beach. What's that even about?*

BLIGHT: *He maketh the storm a calm, and the waves thereof are still....* [1]

The brochure that came in the mail promised a quick return on my investment. There were color photographs of tranquil southern beaches and sidewalks where tourists strolled past fashionable shops and elegant restaurants. A map showed curving streets and geometric lots, rectangular on the straight sections of road, trapezoids around the corners, like pillow cases hanging on a clothesline in the breeze. Some of these plots were crossed out, indicating they were already sold. "You'd better hurry," I said to myself, then laughed and tossed the brochure aside.

last time we went south
for vacation, the wind blew
and stirred up the waves
so hard a man drowned in them
showing he knew how to surf

and right on the dunes
bright houses had been flooded
porch chairs, umbrellas
scattering around the sand
from under seafront porches

on the beach in Spain
they would send down a young boy
to tell us when lunch
was being served. We would then
stroll back through thickening sun

---

1. From Psalm 107:29, in the Bible (King James version)

#76

CARMODY: *Sit down with the animals, pace in the cages with wolves, look into the black eyes of birds, and smile at the monkeys. [Pause.] But, do not laugh.*

BLIGHT: *You will be turned to stone, is that the story?*

I am trying to sort out the various fictional personae that inhabit my brain. For example, there are the serial movie heroes of my youth—Batman, Tarzan, "Wild Bill" Elliot, and the Phantom. Okay, and the Blessed Virgin of my Catholic school days, and Jesus. Spinoza, Descartes, Locke, and Machiavelli—though they live only in books I've read or on tourist plaques in their hometowns—are real to me. Tony the Tiger, Snap, Crackle, and Pop, and Sugar Bear stared back at me over my breakfast bowl. Now, what's weird is that these "ideas" are as real to me as President Kennedy was or Frank Gifford or Sinatra. No wonder we steer shy of philosophy.

how do you know
what's tougher to endure
tender kisses
punches to the solar plexus
or rude looks the other way

we tracked rabbits
in the snow, and saw footprints
of a red fox
where heavy snow covered pines
closed in and blocked our way

can't talk about
the inner yearnings for life
fully human
without fumbling abstractions
or low moans of self-pity

✧

Trained Seals

CARMODY: *I remember Cheetah from the Tarzan movies, how he'd pull his lips back and seemed to smile (or was it a grimace?).*

BLIGHT: *And, he'd pound his chest with hairy hands, yelping that way chimpanzees do.*

Somebody's grandmother, you might have said, or maybe a librarian from San Rafael, except for the pink tulle tutu over padded ski pants and the broad sun hat with a long neck flap. She was sitting with her back against a wall on the San Francisco Embarcadero, her knees pulled up to her chin. She was singing. Beside her on the ground lay a large athletic gear bag, unzipped. Wooden things spilled from it—the handle end of a broken baseball bat, a cane, branches torn from low hanging trees, pieces of old lath, and a two-foot length of half-inch dowel.

She came here every day and sat up her spot opposite the sea lions that gathered on floats a little way out from the pier. She sang; they barked, in syncopation.

"She's part of San Francisco's homeless problem," a man in a Giants sweatshirt said to the small crowd.

"I thought she was hired by the tourist bureau," another man said, and everyone laughed.

"A left-over hippie?" a woman in red asked, expecting laughter too, but everyone just looked at her blankly.

"Where you from?" a Mexican boy asked, sarcastically.

While the sea lions on their floats were the main attraction—cumbering over one another, going in and coming out of the water—it was hard to ignore the singing woman. Her voice became harsher and sharper, the rhythms quicker.

As if she could no longer tolerate the competition from the sea lions, she straightened her legs, kicking the bag of spilled sticks aside, and stood up.

Was she, indeed, a homeless person, I wondered, mentally ill in all likelihood, poverty stricken, and alone in the world; or was she a local eccentric, wealthy as all get out, come down from a fabulous house on Russian Hill or Chinatown, to test the gullibility of denizens and tourists?

"Oh, you idiots," she said to the crowd as she stuffed the sticks back into her bag, then picked it up and walked away toward the Ferry Building. As she disappeared, the crowd turned back to the sea lions.

"When they balance a ball on their noses and toss it to their trainer like in the circus…" a woman in a chartreuse baseball cap and silk hoodie announced, "…when they do that, they call them trained seals."

#79

CARMODY: *What I do not want are any courageous fights with cancer or Alzheimer's. They come for me, I want to be fed, bathed, and rested.*

BLIGHT: *Behind closed doors, with a mountain of submissions on the table, every choice is—weighty.* [Pause.] *You see the connection?*

So, what's wrong with this statement—"the moon gone red under *aurora borealis*, rolled in the dawn's wet grasses?" The image is clear enough; a brightly red-colored sky tints even the moon that's reflected in the dew on the lawn. Does it represent a waste of precious words? When we ask that question, the whole discussion changes. How is it possible to waste words? Is there only a limited supply? And the answer, of course, is contextual. I want to know what specific work the words are supposed to do, besides just getting us onto the right count and over to the next line.

What did he see
exactly? He was looking
so far ahead
holding his breath for long thoughts
changing the subject quickly

senses deranged
the soft connection between
actions and words
dissolves; your words are scattered
to fall to the ground in poems

words stacked like bricks
erect a talking chimney
knocking it down
the words tumble in the field
a poem to capture the eyes

✧

#80

CARMODY: *I started out thinking I'd give them a piece of my mind, but by the time it was my turn to speak, you might say my ardor had cooled. "Oh, nothing," I answered, when they called my name.*

BLIGHT: *Are you trying to say there's no such thing as light without heat?*

I was begging
near my shopping cart and bags
money for food
it said on my old cardboard
sleeping under the freeway

who'd be looking
if the magic curtain fell
revealed the Wizard
not so disillusioning
as no one's being there

it's little things
you wring your hands and listen
disappointment
take it home and cuddle it
makes a personal keepsake

✧

At Carmody's Bar Waiting for Ezra Pound: A Theatrical

(Five Episodes)

3. Up Close and Personal

We were wakened during the night by an argument somewhere inside the hotel, a quarrel between a young man and a young woman. They were speaking Italian, and I could only guess he was supplicant, an offender whose infidelity had apparently put him at risk; he might now lose his love. His voice was deep and soft, modulated by his guilt. She, however, was an angel with beautiful anger, who answered her unfaithful lover with a riot of musical accusation, each note rising to silence his moans, to fill each interstice in his stuttering contrition with a mounting sing-song of logic and clarion verdict. Her voice rode over his, drowning out his laconic sputtering, a dozen or more notes to his one.

CARMODY: *Jesus, man, will you come in out of the rain?*

BLIGHT: *I was just out here listening.*

the translator
of pure sounds hears no words
makes his own way
imposing rhythms, sculpts a tone self
who speaks both for now and then

The woman I was with heard the whole thing differently. She believed the rapidity and pitch of the girl's speech revealed that she was the one who had strayed, and the young man's soft low tones were born of his hurt. When he would gently chide her, it provoked her frantic allegro in defense. She talked fast and loud to silence his accusations, to protest her sham innocence.

CARMODY: *The modern telegraph started it all.* [Snaps his fingers.] *Vital messages across the ocean in the blink of an eye.*

BLIGHT: *When words are whispered from one person to another, fragments will leak out, spill on the floor.*

then they returned
the men from the ships, swarthy
hungry and torn
poets agreed to tell their story
how they had cleaved to the hero

CARMODY: *He was shouting and posturing. Did you see him?*

BLIGHT: *A man of rare parts.*

wild opinions
fill the void, tie us to the mast
lest we succumb
within the gyres of nothingness
subtle confidence of doubt

Next morning on our way to breakfast, we scrutinized everyone below a certain age, looking for our mystery duo. We looked for tiredness in the eyes, a sadness of expression, some sign of pathos or tragedy. We detected nothing. One woman came into the dining room looking exhausted. Ah-ha, we thought, we've nabbed one of them at least, but she was quickly joined by a smiling husband and two very energetic children.

CARMODY: *History is the translation of one set of coordinates into another.*

BLIGHT: *Not "when" so much as "where"... I like it.*

a decent grasp
of Greek, the study of ancient
measures, sweet music
of the spheres, mythology
and you can look straight back

Coda

Suppose someone were to say now: "And I mean into the past, where the truth of the present still breathes, still waits for us to discover it and ourselves. Blow off the dust, crack open the book, sound out the unfamiliar syllables, look for what comes through." We could only laugh, I think. The past is so irretrievably lost to us.

CARMODY: *Even if he comes, who's going to talk to him?* [Pause.] *I can't talk to him.*

BLIGHT: *I'll get him to stand drinks all 'round.*

4. Time, Gentlemen, Time

CARMODY: *What the older man knows. That's my objective.*

BLIGHT: *Don't take too long describing the winds or the leaves that dance along them.*

The same well-paced intentions fail, somehow, to materialize in any more than bright deeds. And nowadays my knees hurt more, and an old bike injury in my left hip has resulted in persistent *meralgia paresthetica*, a numbing pain that creeps in and burns on the top of my thigh.

then you tell the truth
when you shift your focus onto
things that bubble up
from below, stark underneath
you can't stop them coming up

his mouth hangs widely
open, his truths unable
to form themselves
into solid things; they flutter
on the stale wind of his breath

CARMODY: *At the end of a career, he was just taking stock, reading the old stuff over and over.*

BLIGHT: *Dog-eared thin volumes. What a cliché!*

I could barely read up there. I felt out of place. My eyes welled up with rheum and I wiped them on my sleeve.

They were thinking I was so old, I know what they were thinking! Too old to take seriously. They'd listen, they were being forced to listen, but they'd get out of here as quickly as possible.

"Did you hear that old guy?" they'd ask each other. "Jesus! What was that about?"

experience
encrusts the music of the poem
makes it crackle
as the words come out, a brittle
rhythm, the limps and shuffles

that is time spent
and once spent not to be found
again. All the things
I did but can't remember
love slides away like a dream

CARMODY: *We'll ask him back, anyway. How would it look?*

BLIGHT: *Give him something other than top billing. Right?*

A damnation in disguise, if you were to ask me. A person should be allowed to wrap things up, fold his tent, drive on down the road. But, that is not how it works. You admit to yourself or anyone else that you (even maybe) can't perform at the old level, and you are looking death in the face. I mean, right in his cold eyes.

of course, I'll do it
anything not to scuff around
in my slippers
wondering why the meals on wheels
is late dropping off my Styrofoam

CARMODY: *See? I told you. Never too late.*

BLIGHT: *You go in. I'll wait here in the car.*

The poet reads:

lateness of the hour
wears on all of us here. The light
thins, the shadows
are at one with the trees
they're meant to be the shadows of

7. On the Scent

The two professors of modern literature whom Carmody met in the Prince of Wales Bookshop were skeptical. They were of the opinion that Ezra Pound was certainly dead by now, and in more ways than one!

"Even were you able to resurrect the scoundrel," the older one said, "and drag him to your bar, even so, I doubt anyone would come to hear him."

Carmody was struck dumb by the cut of the remark.

"We've come a long way in poetry since Pound's day," the other professor said.

And Carmody was struck deaf by the scandal of the utterance. He ran from the shop holding his ears with both hands.

how long is the life
of deathless poetry? The notes
struck on a golden
bell, the harmonies of wind
rattling winter's leafless limbs

CARMODY: *I take heart from recent sales.* [Pause.] *Personae has flown out the door. That's what I hear.*

BLIGHT: *A murmuration of starlings!*

whose opinion
can with justice now stop up the flow
of poetry
whose lazy eye, whose stunted cadences
muffle the passionate voice

publican, draw me
a flagon of mead, bear honey
for my dry lips
I have come into this ragged place
dragging the comeliest of the gods

Philosophically, it was a question whether Ezra Pound would enter in spirit or in the flesh. Devoted followers, extremists in too many cases, always came with the faint hope of actually meeting the troubadour, to shake his knobby hand. They bore their disappointments with great fortitude; they could not imagine the swing of poetry's history any but downward since the death in Venice of Mauberly, due to an intestinal blockage. But, I digress....

CARMODY: *When he gets here, drinks are on the house.*

BLIGHT: *How about a little something on account?*

they were looking
for reasons to depreciate him
perhaps politics
was something he was lacking. Odd
for one with such a subtle ear

her ear was tin!
we said of Julia's reciting
Yeats's "rise up now"
her Valdosta drawl definitive
she plumbed the meaning the verse

When you listen to them speak—Gertrude Stein, Franklin D. Roosevelt, John L. Lewis, Knute Rockne, Walter Pidgeon, Wallace Stevens, and Katherine Hepburn—all sound strangely and quaintly British, but, at any rate, not American exactly. The same is true of Ezra Pound, even though he was from Idaho. Listen to him read poems aloud:

www.youtube.com/watch?v=-d7-yvs8-JE

CARMODY: *I for one will be conning his poems in my own mind's voice, hearing with the inner ear the craggy beauty, the hard truths.*

BLIGHT: "For the seven lakes, and by no man these verses..."[1] [Pause.] *Yes!*

---

1. From "Canto XLIX" ("The Seven Lakes Canto") by Ezra Pound, *The Fifth Decad of the Cantos XLII–LI* (London: Faber & Faber, 1937)

8. Out of the Fog

A man with a classic gray goatee is leaning with his back to the bar in Carmody's Bar, expatiating on the virtues of Dante. He wears baggy corduroy slacks and an old jacket. His hat lies on the bar. No one is listening, although patrons nod and greet him cheerily as they pass from the bar to their tables with fresh beers. "As I once said to Homer," he pronounces (Homer Loomis Pound was his father), "the thing is rather like, or unlike, subject and response and counter subject in fugue."

The musicality of verse. Perhaps, no one knows who he really is.

CARMODY: *What did I tell you?* [Pause.] *Are we in at the return of Modernism, or what?*

BLIGHT: *I looked a lot like my father. But, I mean, I wasn't the same person as my father.*

pick up the thread
of a zillion vowels and consonants
twist and twirl
in time upon itself, the tones
of a century of verse

line up the words
across an arched stone bridge over
the river *Kiang*
technically, all poems are the same
our mouths and brains in tandem

He wears his erudition on his sleeve, the way another man might wear his sadness.

they are all dead
but this enchanted ghostly poet
back to the bar
recalls "Old Possum" questioning
an anonymous and suspect cheese

They left their poetry behind for us to muse upon, and turned the tide of literature the way cowboys in the movies turned stampeding cattle, round upon themselves, into ever smaller circles. In the post-Modern aftermath, the carefully crafted stream of English language poems ran into the canyon wall and scattered in countless ragged little pieces.

CARMODY: *I am completely reinvigorated! Reinvigorated, I tell you.*

BLIGHT: *Now that your chickens have come home to roost.*

the evening runs
down, as usual, and we forget
there was someone
here. Every night we wait for him
he is the symbol of our fate

someone recites
two longish and obscure poems
Homage to Sextus
Propertius, takes a breath, and then
Sestina: Altaforte

Dream air is thinner than normal air: You hardly know you're breathing. The surfaces of things are blown delicate as a result; you dare not touch them. Be satisfied with imagining he really came this time, and that the rollicking evening was a complete success. We've got to get some of the others next time, though, Ford and Eliot, of course, and Yeats, and I've always wanted to drink across from Henry James.

Don't you think the air's just a little too thin right now?

10. Have We Learned Anything?

Look at me, at myself. I row up to the dock and throw in my line. Who will pick it up, who tie it to the post, stop my drifting with every river.... Look at me, where I wrestle with the imagery of the poet, trying to carve out of myself a song of myself. Every poem the life story of the poet, I mean every poem, every line, every *spondee-dactyl* (one-two and then the three-four) in a shower of beauty. Not what happens in that everyday sense, of the milk, the dough, and the radio, but the inward life of the working poem.

CARMODY: *He can come in here and drink with us anytime.*

BLIGHT: *Any time he wants to, you mean.*

what he teaches
with these metaphorically
oblique passages
the long downhill angle splashed
against our Time's resistances

how we have made
it all up. The gods behind the world
their true meaning
in all fantasy across the sky
say it, say it! In dream images

My every vein and muscle musical, my brain a fiction written in clear prose, certainty draws syllables out, draws the long vowel out, draws out the song under the grammar.

he puts it loosely
wondering if the true ones will come
making a hole
in himself to let the world in
playing its truths like notes on a horn

Keeps a bucket of literate stuff, stuff he's read or heard someone talk about. The stuff spills out on his page. Is that right?

CARMODY: *Do you think anyone still reads the* Cantos?

BLIGHT: *It saddens me to think we might have turned onto another road.*

But, my life is so ordinary, so like all the others. What if I recorded everything that was important, and what if I got it exactly right?

How deep would I have to go?

when he looked up
the whole flow of tragic imagery
locked directly
onto the day-to-day rhythms
of my ordinary life, boring

really. But the words
can color and enliven it
paint other truths
over the bad spots, the worms
where the rot works through

see if I can
make myself look straight at the sore
and still think about
making it better. All that's human
authenticates whatever song

CARMODY: *Is this the ending then?*

BLIGHT: *Do you know the Greek for that?*

End of the Line

CARMODY: [Has come to a wooden barrier in his path. He stops and peers over it, down into a hole.] *Do you think this is the end of the line?*

BLIGHT: Détour, *as the French say, a change of direction.* [Pause.] *Or, maybe we're supposed to go a little deeper, you know, get down below the surfaces.*

✧

#81: Pushing the Paint Around

CARMODY: *Do you know what depresses me? It's that I'm not more depressed. Yes, that's right. I need* angst *if I'm ever going to write serious poetry.*

BLIGHT: *Climb up on your pain. How far can you see?*

It was just before Christmas, 1959, and Pete Schnitzler and I were bunking in the student government offices while we finished our senior theses. I was typing away on my land-use survey of western Riverside County, but Pete was completing a final painting show. He brought in a dozen "canvases" (they were thin Lauan sheets nailed to wooden frames), a stepladder, cans and tubes of paint, brushes, and rollers. He gesso'd all the frames, and then, one by one, systematically created his "abstractions." In a couple of cases, he threw paint at them. For another two or three, he climbed up the ladder and poured different colors of paint onto the plywood. He drew squares over squares and circles and pushed the paint around with the roller and drew rough swaths across them with the brushes. When he had finished, he leaned them against the walls all around the office. What a show!

genetically
art comes from the same sources
as height and weight
we always think we're steering
the boat, as waves hoist us up

peering inward
darkness has an ache to it
against a wall
we're losing all energy
bits of idea just fizzle

by accident
someone complains because
nothing goes right
urgently, to make it known
we need to show everything

Along the Gallery Wall: A Review

CARMODY: *Kandinsky, Mondrian, Paul Klee, Hans Hoffman... these are your true realists.*

BLIGHT: *Now, that really is Platonic!*

1

Four small square paintings on a wall about eye level in a row from left to right and subtly colored.

it is not in words
they speak, the colors reaching

The first, composed of flattened blackened squares that yearn across the gap to grasp an idea of umber fountains in the second.

mute and hopelessly
rooted between black and orange

The fountain in its own corner, stretching backwards after orange swaths as for a breath of air, overwrought and threatening to fall out of the frame.

explosions in the next

2

On the farthest right, like a flag on fire, a white band breaks out from rough-brushed reds. The center blocked in its regress by thick filigrees of orange and green on the left.

no bridging that gap
the green waits like a spider

Even though a complicated story of wingéd fairies etched in soft pastels and petals framed in still more black is urgent from the farther side of that.

the story burgeons

The palest blue weeping onto gray is anchored either side of pictures two and three and the whole of two is harmony, an easy percolation up through pale cream and sandy colorations.

till a bridge is carefully
pitched across the open air

3

black is heavier
and weighs the left end down

That is the first canvas and the darkest one, a seething overlay obstructing something fainter, far more distant, lighter.

a tarred obliteration

Its explicit meaning hidden—I imagine some graffiti artist's moniker in scroll buried under overlapping swatches of streaky black and gray put on with a roller.

at the start. Forward from that
the whole folds into the void

✧

#82

CARMODY: *If you want to know, I'm simply bored.*

BLIGHT: *I shouldn't know too much, if I were you.*

If you take two common nouns, let's say *hammer* and *nail*, and an abstract word like *nearness*, for example, and then, thinking of them all together, force the choice of a distant verb, like *eases*, we could, poetically speaking, get a line, then, like this—*hammer eases the nail of nearness*. But, continuing in this exiguous vein, what's to prevent either "love of wisdom & love of sun compelling elevations" or "nearly energized, the wikiup, house basket"? The pangs of hunger ride roller coasters, roller coasters of—what? Tied up boring with a string. A world of poetry newly opened when the type cases were overturned and the dingbats spilled all over the floor.

the fusion of
more than momentary thuds
not only words
intersect, but also where
the tree bends to the cold wind

what I had seen
still was not named, was up
to me to call
the nomad determined, dub
the niceties of slaughter

from the nothing
we are free to this extent
we are an edge
of a living, growing thing
much depends on how we choose

✧

#83

CARMODY: *I'm so sick of people talking, talking, talking as if no one was listening.*

BLIGHT: *We're all salesmen now, I heard, subject to pure market forces.*

The dramaturge hurries forward, he can't act at all, but he sure can talk. Cordelia gets her lines all wrong; "Stop, stop," he demands, coming out from the wings. He speaks of fathers and daughters, then, how such love is always so ambiguous. The frailty of father, old and feathery, going slightly mad. Life, he had bestowed in his own mind, they all owed very life to him. We all understand that! But, once our own hand is on the sack of gold there's no letting go. "Sadder," I think he meant, "play it sadder."

not everyone
can have a mother who hanged
herself for sins
and left the crumpled body
there for you to stumble on

it's hard to grieve
when you're all by yourself
and harder yet
to tell in great detail
where the true thorns are stuck

✧

Eight Episodes in the Saga of Carmody & Blight

1.

Peter Carmody, wise beyond knowing,
took up pencil and a paper pad to write
the Poem of His Life, not
his best poem, but his life's story.

First thing Peter noticed was that his mind
would not neatly put things in a row.
Memories came to him like silver salmon
leaping up the falls; he clutched at them
the way he'd seen a Grizzly do (in a film),
trying to catch something for starters.

2.

Peter met Andrew Blight in a mirror
shaving, but didn't recognize the chin
at first. The mole so like his own.
So, Peter leaned in closer.

Conversation was easy with Blight;
he seemed to run ahead and know Peter's
every thought, always ready to agree.
When he did find fault, he would only
raise an eyebrow and cluck with his tongue.
Peter was glad for a friend.

3.

It was late summer when they met
and they often took long probing walks together,
asking and answering those questions that
for so long bothered Peter,

questions of the weight of truth,
the vacuity of love, how popularity was bought.
Andrew knew Peter's heart like his own,
and he shared his secrets,
how one had to hide one's feelings;
go along, you know, to get along.

4.

Peter Carmody alone left him to be
desired, a hole where Blight now figured
to fill up, a well-rounded personality.
He crept out now where he had hid.

And had opinions for the very first time,
about Art, for Christ's sake, and cuisine.
When he woke, Carmody, he first looked
around for his new friend
and often found him in the loo
tending to his ablutions.

5.

Blight, tripping, alludes how he had found
Carmody lacking at first, but now
has all the confidence. "The world is
a funny place," he started saying.

They now revel in twin bright suns.
Have become inseparable.
When one was not there, the other pined.
"I need him to feel whole," they said,
remarking how the other blended in.
Now they bathed and shaved together.

6.

Peter Carmody looked him in the eye,
in the mirror, and asked whether
Blight was plotting something, the way
he just happened to come into

Carmody's life. He could see Blight was
his spitting image and puzzled
were they brothers and shared the same genome;
had he got his nose the same place Peter had?
But then, as the image smiled cheerfully,
Carmody picked up his razor and began to shave.

7.

A hardest time for Carmody
came introducing Blight
among his closest friends. He worried
how the other's brusquer

manner came across. How was he understood?
Carmody could hardly keep himself
from elbowing in to clarify
the wilder things Blight was likely to say.
Still, he sunned himself
in the other one's audacity.

8.

Straining to keep poles apart, Carmody
disconnected, pushed against his image
in the mirror, blinked for focus,
watched psychologically,

saw off and on, the one and the other;
called him, "Andrew? It is Andrew?"
Stared him down in the glass reflections,
tried to wipe him off in the steam.
But all Andrew's image did was stare
back at him, the eyes somewhat off kilter.

✧

Crossroads

CARMODY: *You see that? Fifty cars or more, all with their headlights on. Some dignitary's funeral?*

BLIGHT: *Or some other kind of parade.*

lingering rain
now its wildest rhythms
slowed—*direct me, Lord*
ta-dum, ta-dum—a tedium
at the blackened lychgate

No funeral today, but it's not like nobody has died. News circulates from all corners of the dying world—of murder, accident, disease, and thousands lost in a flood, gone overboard, or starved. Life struggles on against the dying, against the cold statistics of despair.

sad, sad, Columbine
raw combination of dove
and eagle's talon
delicately blue and white
uncomprehending star

night lay frozen
in a sullen graying hush
thuds and scratching gone
I hoped to talk to the moon
when it finally appeared

The stars are nearly out, flamboyant, lustrous in a sky made obviously of arched Plexiglas. And the wind is blowing hard down here against the slinky yielding trees, the trees glad for the exercise now their leaves have dropped, and the leaves skip and swirl, dancing for all the world.

then the rain tires
lets angled sweeps of sunlight
fall overwrought
across strewn muddy puddles
down from the littlest twigs

and again silence
threatens to invade the sad
rhythms of the dead
slowed to stop—*direct me, Lord*
ta-dum, ta-dum, a tedium

Gratefully, I was walking back from the grave, sending my thoughts to any other place, urging them away, when it abruptly ceased to rain. The tree bark soaked was darker now, and the lawn sparkled in the wet as if baskets of shattered glass had spilled, but either no one noticed or all were so gorged with emotion they could not muster more.

the plain fact of it
there has to be an end
to death and dying
for the living to get on
with the little that is left

that storm withdrew
while sheets of the yellow sun
snapped over the lawns
like the new-making of a bed
or a table festive set

comes hopeful sunshine
to guy our long sad faces

He bent over there at the edge of the cemetery and picked something up. "What did you find," his brother asked, walking along, "the end of a string?" "The end of something," he answered, "we'll have to see where it leads."

I hawk out—*direct me, Lord*
ta-dum, ta-dum—a tedium
quit at the blackened lychgate

Part IV

A Dozen Dialogues on Dying

—in memory of Jim Percey

    he taught them all
    the pleasures of the kitchen
    how to think past
    sacred barriers, piled crap
    tell the truth, feint with your right

          […]

CARMODY: *This place is like a hospital. How can we liven things up?*

BLIGHT: *Some vignettes from the old Paris days?*

::

CARMODY: *We are thirsts slackened, you and I, something now over with, if you get my drift.*

BLIGHT: *Draw us another anyway.*

✧

#84

CARMODY: *It's taken such a long time to grow this old, but that seems beside the point now.*

BLIGHT: *Marching to the end. We're always on the march.*

On the telephone I learn between sobs and caught breaths that my oldest friend is being moved to hospice—do I want to come and see him? When he left California decades ago to return to Pennsylvania to teach, I drove all night down from Berkeley to Long Beach to say goodbye to him, and he was waiting on his front porch for me with a pitcher of Manhattans. I will not make this trip now, however, partly because I am afraid it would undermine a lifetime's memories, but, mainly, because I don't think I could stand it.

it's always now
in this dance of memories
macabre turnings
in a black wind, around
our eyes persistent gnats

the past has gone
before us, all that's left
remembering
each fraction as whispered
happening a given day

dead in my eyes
his life memorialized
what little's left
I throw my heart at clouds
on the wind going east

✧

#85

CARMODY: *I'm afraid of blood, the sight, even the very idea, of blood.* [Pause.] *Red, I love red, however.*

BLIGHT: *Colors and their quick associations: black as night, perhaps, but I think right away of blood in the stool.*

Down in the village the roads are clogged with cars, like sick arteries. Up here in the hills the roads are empty and quiet—rainless ruts, teeth in a buried head. The sun is shining; the breezes make the branches sway; day sits right down upon us. Sounds of life come from far away, nothing up close.

my head pulses
to the crowding up of things
a dead squirrel
in the road, the ravenous
tentative crows hopping

a faucet drips
its watery *bolero*
in all the rooms
bad thoughts come marching
to its flimsy drumbeat

with a raw joke
and a crude cartoon of Death's
head, black on white
we try to keep on laughing
at jokes about *abattoirs*

✧

#86

CARMODY: *Life and death, immortality and hereafter—I see in them manifest the way day ends, the gradual attenuation of the light, the cool coming in of darkness.* [Satisfied.]

BLIGHT: *If only we could see in the dark.* [Pause.] *Are you afraid of the dark?*

"We'll find out soon enough," the philosopher said. The argument had been about whether we could know if there was an afterlife, and I had said, "How could there be? Has anyone ever come back from the dead?" Sister Mary Bridget turned to me and asked: "Does an assertion without proof have the same logical standing as the doubt that questions it?" She laughed, then gave a quick wave with her hand, and pulled an egg out of my ear.

in a wren's eye
as I held him in my hand
I saw our deaths
a tiny light flickered out
shiny dark surfaces dulled

it's metaphor
you see (even when you don't)
in the darkness
with a magical black light
edges fade to shadows

when you're sleeping
or anesthetized you're still
exactly where?
coming in or going out
time just has no meaning

✧

#87

CARMODY: *Do you know the worst thing? No? Well, I'll tell you. The worst thing is how you feel guilty when someone you know is dying…you just feel terrible.*

BLIGHT: *Imagine how they feel.*

Take any newspaper…how many obituaries every day? Ten? Fifty? My God, look at *The New York Times*. And of all the people who die, how many even get into the paper? Or think about India or Africa. Dying all over the place—dying, dying, dying. It's enough to make you sick.

in hospitals
they wash their hands so often
you'd think the skin
might come off—*"Out, damned spot! Out!"*
plague's most hermetic question

how would you like
to be the oncologist
that cancer guy
looking death right in the eye
behind his prognoses

it's like a lake
these rivers flow into it
and they flow out
humanity's the wide spot
where the ebb and flow slow down

✧

#88

CARMODY: *What must seem enormous to the person dying, i.e., the fact of their dying, can often seem trivial to others. [Pause.] Maybe we only take it for granted that it seems so significant to the one who is dying.*

BLIGHT: *If I were to say, "it all depends," I know you would just ask me, "depends on what?"*

We always hear that dying is part of living. Think about that. Dying just comes up like, say, my needing to urinate or feeling hungry. You're walking along or just sitting somewhere, and dying shows up; I mean, it just comes along, and so you do it?

the mystery
returns, once they're in the grave
where did they go?
they're not present anymore
they must have gone someplace

why did he go
gently, no burning, no rage
what did he feel
as it came up on him
as it entered into him

it's like hearing
about a toothache. You can't
experience
the sharp, hard, cold nail of it
deeply crippling spasms

✧

#89

CARMODY: *In a moment bright as a bubble in the middle of a sunny Saturday, I thought about dying. It was quite strange, of course.*

BLIGHT: *But it's not uncommon.* [Pause.] *Why don't we ever say, "I'm absolutely living to get out of here," for example, the way we say, "I'm dying to meet her"?*

Each day that I stay away from my old friend who is dying in hospice, I feel a little guiltier. He is probably having some good days, even some really lucid moments, but I know that as soon as I arrived there would be moans of pain and a wild blathering that would break my heart. I do not belong in this phase of his life. I wouldn't want him healthy and articulate hanging around my deathbed.

don't remind me
how unpleasant the world is
sad all around
I'm struggling to explicate
my attachment to it

I let my eye
loose to sail into the sky
it fled the world
stretched clouds along the wind
refusing to answer me

parallel lives
against the threatened losses
silence, immobility
the living and the dying
rub themselves raw

✧

#90

CARMODY: *Death and his desperate little partners—sickness, accident, and fortuity—are coming around a lot these days, you hear more about them, see them sometimes just ducking into an alley, speeding away in a big black car.*

BLIGHT: *That was beautiful.*

Here's a metaphor. A powerful, sudden, multi-colored, shimmering idea comes to you, a strong reverberating image, and you shake your head, rub your eyes, and get to work. You write a poem, a piece of intense and perfectly crafted verse—you think modestly of Stevens, Williams, Wilbur, and Bidart. So, you type it up and submit it to *Poetry, The Sewanee Review, The New Yorker, Ploughshares*, and *The Paris Review*. One by one the slips come back in the mail, each expressing the editor's sincere regret at the death of your precious poem.

a call at night
she's had another stroke
your poor mother
remembers her manners
gracious and dignified

old love letters
forgotten in a box
there is a name
but no recollection who
wrote such clichéd feelings

how far ahead
can symptoms telegraph
a deadly threat
some small cough in the night
slightly dizzy at the store

✧

#91

CARMODY: *If I were dying, I wouldn't want to know it. Just let the music play, pour the wine, and then come and call me just before the sun comes up.*

BLIGHT: *Out of sight, out of mind?*

CARMODY: [Explaining patiently.] *If you can't escape death, you can at least make it as small a part of life as possible.*

I cannot get any nearer the truth here; my eyes are glazing over. Dear God, why are these things kept so secret? I lean in to kiss Death, but Death is painted roughly black, it is large and black, and square—a whole wall of black. Is it a picture? I can't think my way out of this!

God does no work
the universe twirls freely
we live and die
as birds fall from the wires
as light slides to darkness

a memory
she once was fat and living
an old woman
disappeared down a hole
I just vaguely remember

they'll think of me
I think now of them thinking
of me for aye
where did the hours go
all that's left is the waiting

✧

#92

CARMODY: *What interests me is the way my remembering some unimportant event, like dinner at a restaurant with him, trumps for a moment the certain knowledge that he is right now suffering.*

BLIGHT: *Maybe we just live in a dream world.*

I did not know anyone who died in school. After that, there were a few kids from college who died later in Viet Nam, but no one I knew closely. Relatives, older people, were, of course, dying all along the way. It wasn't until I had been working several years in Upstate New York that people I actually knew began dying around me, but most of these were still older, just names in their obituaries. In the last few years, though, people of my generation have begun dropping like flies.

I think of ghosts
dreams and memories of dead
acquaintances
can it really be over
for them, just blank pages

death distanced
from breathing, feeling quick
cold cadavers
never can experience
lament, the cleansing sobs

they come in dreams
dead faces, muttering
stings your conscience
you get up in the night
Scotch in a glass of milk

✧

#93

CARMODY: *Did you ever think—"Hey, it could be me. I might be next"?*

BLIGHT: *You mean like, any minute? [Pause.] I think I prefer not to think about it.*

Everyone has plans, right? We work out an ideal future and then we design strategies that will carry us from situation to situation and, finally, to our goal. We think this way about everything, from planning our kids' education to National Defense Policy. The truth is, however, that logic outstrips our capacity to exert control, and unanticipated events are forever interfering and setting entirely different sequences into play. I met my second wife, the mother of two of my children and the source of my happiness for nearly thirty years, entirely by accident. She was no part of any plan of mine.

hypothesis
experimentation
and revision
we're lost in the subtleties
of whatever could have been

you always guess
wrong, even when the outcome
appears to fit
you've fallen from the window
but walked away unhurt

my causal sense
leads me to speculate
maybe the phone
itself guides death through its night
Virgil led Dante through hell

✧

#94

CARMODY: *Death is so final it erases all the worry leading up to it.*

BLIGHT: *No mourning? No ritual laments? No wailing?*

CARMODY: *Lift your voices!*

So, I got the call this afternoon. My dear old friend has died. I expected to be grief-stricken, but I'm not. I'm free now to remember him, to lean again on the bar at *Das Gasthaus* from noon to 2:00 A.M. or to arrive again at his farm for dinner after a long January drive, and to resume the political argument from four months before. His death disencumbers the future (however long that will be for me). His impending death had me stalled, stuck on a sickening fear, but his son says in an email that he had come to accept dying and was at peace with it. Put away your tears!

a single life
run through to its conclusion
has new meaning
"now against threatened losses
silence, immobility"

he taught them all
the pleasures of the kitchen
how to think past
sacred barriers, piled crap
tell the truth, feint with your right

death punctuates
that's my very last word
exclamation
point sometimes, a period
ampersand, *et cetera*

✧

Quietus

CARMODY: *It seems as if every generation has to rediscover that it's death that makes living inestimable.*

BLIGHT: *You never know what you've got till you've lost it.*

I came to the farm where my oldest friend had lived and where he died. I had come for the burying of his ashes. People stood or sat around in little groups on the lawn or under the big maple. I walked past them, up on the porch, and into the house. As I went through the front door I all but expected to see him there in his kitchen. Old conversations around the kitchen table were playing in my mind and I felt him there. But of course, he wasn't there. I catch myself sometimes thinking I should call him, but never make it all the way to the phone.

he's not anywhere
now and the memories fade
to become just words
I tell all the old stories
but no pictures come to mind

sometimes he's shown up
in my dreams, not exactly
acting like himself
he'll say things I never heard
stand there uncomfortably

I tipped his ashes
in the Liffey and they made
a cloud that drifted
down to the river, sinking
slowly as if saying goodbye

✧

End Notes

that is time spent
and once spent not to be found
again. All the things
I did but can't remember
love slides away like a dream

[…]

CARMODY: *The now is difficult, you know? Come right up to it—it slithers away. Look back upon it—it shrugs its shoulders and curls its lip. There just isn't any—now.*

BLIGHT: *What were we doing this exact same time yesterday?*

✧

About the Author

Charles D. Tarlton holds a Ph.D. in political philosophy/American history from UCLA and is a retired university professor of political theory who lives in Massachusetts with his wife, Ann Knickerbocker, an abstract painter. After retiring in 2006, he began writing poetry and flash fiction. His work has appeared in a number of print and online venues, including *Abramalin, Atlas Poetica, Barnwood, Blue and Yellow Dog, Contemporary Haibun Online, Cricket Online Review, Haibun Today, Houston Literary Review, Inner Art Journal, KYSO Flash, Linden Avenue Literary Journal, Peacock Journal, Prune Juice, Rattle, Red Booth Review, Shot Glass, Six-Minute Magazine, Skylark,* and *Ink, Sweat & Tears*, among others. He is also the author of these works:

1. *Get Up and Dance,* a collection of tanka-prose "dance poems" (KYSO Flash Press, 2019), with cover art by Ann Knickerbocker and still photos, in color, from videos and films of dance-works

2. *Touching Fire: New and Selected Ekphrastic Prosimetra* (KYSO Flash Press, 2018), a unique collection of more than 50 hybrid prose/poetry works created in response to fine artworks, 47 of which appear in full color in the book:
   http://www.kysoflash.com/Books.aspx#Fire

3. *Una Vida de Piedra y de Palabra* (twelve improvisations on Pablo Neruda's *The Heights of Macchu Picchu*), Number 23 in the 2River Chapbook Series, which features the author reading three sections aloud (II: Truth in the Larger Sense; IV: On Death, and Dying's Threshold; and XII: *Ecce Homo*):
   http://www.2river.org/chapbooks/tarlton/default.html

   The chapbook is also available in PDF, with cover art by Ann Knickerbocker:
   http://www.2river.org/chapbooks/tarlton/book/tarlton.pdf

4. "The Turn of Art," a drama in verse and prose which pits Picasso against Matisse, in *Fiction International* (Issue 45, Fall 2012): https://fictioninternational.sdsu.edu/wordpress/catalog/issue-45-about-seeing/

5. "Episodes in the Navajo Degradation: A Five-Poem Sequence" in *Lacuna: A Journal of Historical Fiction* (15 April 2012): http://lacunajournal.blogspot.com/2012/04/episodes-in-navajo-degradation-five.html

6. "*Five Lines Down*: An Interesting Moment in the History of Tanka in English" in *Atlas Poetica* (Number 12, Summer 2012), pages 59-70. This analytical essay focuses on the seminal tanka journal of the 1990s, which published only four issues. Tarlton dives "deep into the poetry and essays of the short-lived journal, [and] urges us to give up the clichéd, sentimental, and obvious in favor of deeper truths, originality, and the unique assets of the English language" (M. Kei, *Atlas Poetica*, Number 12; quoted with his permission):
http://www.atlaspoetica.org/wp-content/uploads/2019/05/12-Atlas-Poetica-Journal-of-World-Tanka-poetry.pdf

Credits

Footnotes herein were compiled by Clare MacQueen, with the exception of two Author's notes (pages 33 and 63).

This book contains 130 works, with a total of 146 Carmody & Blight dialogues. These include eight that are un-numbered (one each on the title and dedication pages, and others to introduce each Part of this book), as well as two dozen which are collected within three separate works ("Conundrum," "Talking to Myself," and *At Carmody's Bar Waiting for Ezra Pound: A Theatrical*).

A number of works were published previously, some in slightly different versions, and are reprinted herein with author's permission. Details follow:

Page 11: Tanka verse "in the kitchen" is from Dialogue #15 (pg. 32 herein).

Page 12: Dialogue *"You know, sometimes my moods..."* is reprinted from Tarlton's story "La Folie a Deux" published at *Story Shack* (date unknown): https://thestoryshack.com/flash-fiction/suspense/charles-d-tarlton-la-folie-a-deux/

Page 13: "By the Light of the Moon" first appeared, in a slightly different version, at *postcardshorts.com: stories that fit on a postcard* (23 April 2013): http://www.postcardshorts.com/read-1077.html

Pages 14–16: Dialogues 1–3 were published previously, with different prose sections, in *Sketchbook: A Journal for Eastern & Western Short Forms* (Volume 6, Number 6; November/December 2011).

Pages 20 and 21: Dialogues 7 and 8, in slightly different versions, were published previously in *Blue & Yellow Dog* (Issue 9, Summer 2012): http://blueyellowdog.weebly.com/uploads/4/2/6/3/4263842/blue_yellow_dog_9_summer_issue.pdf

Page 22: "Allusory" is reprinted from *Inner Art Journal* (February 2014): https://innerartjournal.com/featured-poets-february-2014/charles-tarlton/

Page 25: Dialogue #9, in a slightly different version, was published previously in *Blue & Yellow Dog* (Issue 9, Summer 2012).

Page 27: Dialogue #11 appeared previously in *Contemporary Haibun Online* (Vol. 8, No. 1, April 2012) and is reprinted in *Touching Fire: New and Selected Ekphrastic Prosimetra* by Charles D. Tarlton (KYSO Flash Press, 2018).

Page 50: "Crépescule" is reprinted from *Short-Story.Me!* (unknown date): https://www.short-story.me/stories/fantasy-stories/803-crepescule

Page 54: Dialogue #30 is reprinted from *Ink, Sweat & Tears* (11 March 2012): http://www.inksweatandtears.co.uk/pages/?p=100

Pages 55, 56, and 60: Slightly different versions of Dialogues 31–33 were published previously in *Cricket Review Online* (Volume VIII, Issue 1): http://www.cricketonlinereview.com/vol8no1/1-charles-tarlton-carmody-blight-dialogues-31.php

Page 57: Tanka verse "unrelenting" is from Dialogue #47 (pg. 76 herein).

Page 58: Dialogue "*I got right up on the stage...*" is reprinted from Section 2 ("The Italian Model") of *At Carmody's Bar Waiting for Ezra Pound: A Theatrical*, first published in *Atlas Poetica* (Number 31, January 2018): http://www.atlaspoetica.org/wp-content/uploads/2019/06/31-Atlas-Poetica-Journal-of-World-Tanka-poetry.pdf

Page 67: Dialogue "*The great unknown!...*" is reprinted from Section 2 of "Questions Asked in Ignorance: Reflections on Johannes Climacus's Philosophical Fragments," in *Atlas Poetica* (Number 12, Summer 2012): http://www.atlaspoetica.org/wp-content/uploads/2019/05/12-Atlas-Poetica-Journal-of-World-Tanka-poetry.pdf

Page 67: Dialogue "*I woke from a dream...*" is reprinted from "After Roethke," which was published in *Blackbox Manifold* (Issue 14, Spring 2015): http://www.manifold.group.shef.ac.uk/issue14/CharlesTarltonBM14.html

Page 67: Dialogue "*I am not familiar with any Roman poets...*" is reprinted from Section 6 ("On Some Threshold") of *At Carmody's Bar Waiting for Ezra Pound: A Theatrical*, in *Atlas Poetica* (Number 31, January 2018)

Page 67: Dialogue *"Life's gamble: risking everything..."* is from an unpublished section ("9. A Matter of Conscience") of Tarlton's *At Carmody's Bar Waiting for Ezra Pound: A Theatrical.*

Page 84: "A Question of Murder" is reprinted from *KYSO Flash* (Issue 8, August 2017): http://www.kysoflash.com/Issue8/TarltonQuestion.aspx

Page 97: "Psychotherapeutics" is reprinted from *Blackbox Manifold* (Issue 14, 2015):
http://www.manifold.group.shef.ac.uk/issue14/CharlesTarltonBM14.html

Page 99: Tanka verse "senses deranged" is from Dialogue #79 (pg. 133 herein).

Page 100: Dialogue *"You have to get their attention..."* is reprinted from Section 5 of "Questions Asked in Ignorance: Reflections on Johannes Climacus's *Philosophical Fragments,*" in *Atlas Poetica* (No. 12, Summer 2012).

Page 102: "Stereotypicals" is from Tarlton's essay "Thoughts on Tanka Prose," published previously in *Skylark: A Tanka Journal* (Summer 2015).

Page 107: The following dialogues are reprinted from "Questions Asked in Ignorance: Reflections on Johannes Climacus's *Philosophical Fragments,*" in *Atlas Poetica* (Number 12, Summer 2012):

> From Section 6: *"My father told me, 'Just do what you want..."*
> From Section 8: *"I woke up from my nap today..."*
> From Section 4: *"Do you remember when you first became aware..."*
> From Section 3: *"Have you looked to see if there's another way out..."*
> From Section 1: *"How far up the road can we push this wagon..."*

Pages 110–113: "Richard Diebenkorn: Three Ekphrastic Moments" was first published in *Haibun Today* (Volume 9, Number 2, June 2015).

Page 125: "By Their Fruits" is reprinted from *Mad Swirl* (20 August 2013):
http://madswirl.com/short-stories/2013/08/by-their-fruits/

Page 127: "From the Doctor's Rough Drafts" is reprinted from *Atlas Poetica* (Number 37, Summer 2019).

Page 131: "Trained Seals" is reprinted from *Apocrypha and Abstractions* (Volume III, Flash Fiction Musings for the Literary Minded; 29 August 2013): https://apocryphaandabstractions.wordpress.com/2013/08/29/trained-seals-by-charles-tarlton/

Page 135: Four of the five episodes within *At Carmody's Bar Waiting for Ezra Pound: A Theatrical* ["3. Up Close and Personal," "4. Time, Gentlemen, Time," "7. On the Scent," and "8. Out of the Fog"] are reprinted from *Atlas Poetica* (Number 31, January 2018).

Page 150: "Along the Gallery Wall: A Review" appeared previously in *Blackbox Manifold* (Issue 14, 2015):
http://www.manifold.group.shef.ac.uk/issue14/CharlesTarltonBM14.html

Page 158: "Crossroads" is reprinted from *Atlas Poetica* (Issue 18, Summer 2014): https://doc.uments.com/s-atlas-poetica.pdf

Page 161: Tanka verse "he taught them all" is quoted from Dialogue #94 (pg. 173 herein), which was published previously in *Haibun Today* (Volume 6, Number 2, June 2012).

Page 162: Dialogue *"This place is like a hospital…"* is reprinted from Section 5 ("Open Mic") of *At Carmody's Bar Waiting for Ezra Pound: A Theatrical*, first published in *Atlas Poetica* (Number 31, January 2018).

Page 162: Dialogue *"We are thirsts slackened…"* is reprinted from Section 1 ("Home Is the Sailor") of *At Carmody's Bar Waiting for Ezra Pound: A Theatrical*, first published in *Atlas Poetica* (Number 31, January 2018).

Pages 163–173: Dialogues 84 thru 94 were published previously under the title of "Eleven Dialogues on Dying" in *Haibun Today* (Volume 6, Number 2, June 2012):
http://haibuntoday.com/ht62/tp_tarlton_elevendialogues.html

Page 174: "Quietus" is reprinted from *Contemporary Haibun Online* (July 2017, Volume 13, Number 2):
https://contemporaryhaibunonline.com/pages132/Tarlton_Quietus.html

Page 175: Tanka verse "that is time spent" is quoted from "4. Time, Gentlemen, Time" (pg. 137 herein), which is reprinted from *At Carmody's Bar Waiting for Ezra Pound: A Theatrical*, first published in *Atlas Poetica* (Number 31, January 2018).

Page 176: Dialogue *"The now is difficult, you know…"* is reprinted from Section 7 of "Questions Asked in Ignorance: Reflections on Johannes Climacus's *Philosophical Fragments*," in *Atlas Poetica* (No. 12, Summer 2012).

Visual Images

Front and Back Covers: Background image, *Wisps Surrounding the Horsehead Nebula*, is copyrighted © 2012 by SSRO, Star Shadows Remote Observatory. All rights reserved. Image is reproduced with kind permission from Rick Gilbert, SSRO co-founder and webmaster. Image was downloaded from NASA's Astronomy Picture of the Day (9 September 2012): https://apod.nasa.gov/apod/ap120909.html

Title Page Image: *Hail Caesar* (photographer unknown) depicts five "Romans" in 1957, college students who were cheerleaders at the University of California, Riverside (UCR). At far right stands Charles D. Tarlton (known in those days as Chuck Tarlton). The photograph is reproduced in this book with permission from the author, who provided the image from UCR's 1957 yearbook, *The Tartan* (page 31).

Back Cover and Page 184: The KYSO Flash logo is copyrighted © 2015 by Clare MacQueen and was designed in collaboration with James Fancher. All rights reserved.

Permissions

Except for short quotations within critical articles or reviews, no portion of this book (including its covers) may be used, reproduced, or transmitted in any form or by any means, electronic or mechanical, including photocopying, or by any information storage or retrieval system, without permission in writing from the individual copyright holders.

✧ ✧ ✧

About the Publisher

Clare MacQueen served as webmaster and copy editor for 18 issues of *Serving House Journal*, from its launch online in 2010 to its retirement in 2018. She co-edited *Steve Kowit: This Unspeakably Marvelous Life* (Serving House Books, 2015). She's also co-editor, webmaster, and publisher of *KYSO Flash*, the literary journal and micro-press that she founded in 2014 to celebrate a smorgasbord of short-form writings and visual art. Via KYSO Flash Press, she has custom-designed and produced 18 books, including anthologies and collections for writers and artists whose works have been published in *KYSO Flash* online. Her own essays, reviews, stories, and poems have appeared in, among others, *New Flash Fiction Review, Ribbons, Serving House Journal, Skylark,* and in the anthologies *Best New Writing 2007* (Hopewell Publications) and *Winter Tales II: Women on the Art of Aging* (Serving House Books, 2012).

www.kysoflash.com

*an online literary journal &
a micro-press of printed books*

Knock-Your-Socks-Off Art and Literature

KYSO Flash is a trademark registered ® 2014 by Clare MacQueen. The KYSO Flash logo is copyrighted © 2015 by Clare MacQueen and was designed in collaboration with James Fancher. All rights reserved.

www.ingramcontent.com/pod-product-compliance
Lightning Source LLC
Chambersburg PA
CBHW051546010526
44118CB00022B/2603